MÉRIDA

JOSÉ Mª ÁLVAREZ MARTÍNEZ
JOSÉ LUIS DE LA BARRERA ANTÓN
AGUSTÍN VELÁZQUEZ JIMÉNEZ

everest

Editorial Management: Raquel López Varela

Editorial Coordination: Eva María Fernández

Text: José Mª Álvarez Martínez, José Luis de la Barrera Antón, Agustín Velázquez Jiménez

Photographs: Manuel de la Barrera Ocaña, Imagen M.A.S., Archivo Everest

Diagrams: Gerardo Rodera

Translation: Babyl Traducciones

Cartography: © Everest

SECOND EDITION
© José Mª Álvarez Martínez,
   José Luis de la Barrera Antón,
   Agustín Velázquez Jiménez
   EDITORIAL EVEREST, S. A.
Carretera León – A Coruña, km 5 - LEÓN
ISBN: 978-84-241-0618-8
Legal deposit: LE. 507-2010
Printed in Spain

EDITORIAL EVERGRÁFICAS, S. L.
Carretera León – A Coruña, km 5
LEÓN (Spain)

··· MÉRIDA ···

HISTORICAL INTRODUCTION

The most ancient remains found in Mérida and the surrounding area date back to Lower Palaeolithic times. It wasn't until the end of the Neolithic period, however, that these lands were proved to be truly occupied. From these times, around 3000-2000 BC are the remains of a small settlement on the present Avenida de Juan Carlos I, which was almost completely destroyed by a Roman necropolis, also established here, almost three thousand years later.

Stone materials from the Municipal Prehistory Collection.

Excavations of similar settlements from this period have been made in the area around Mérida which indicate the area's significant importance towards the end of the Neolithic and Chalcolithic or Copper Age: Cueva de la Charneca, Araya, La Palecina, etc.

The most outstanding prehistoric monument however, is the *Dolmen de Lácara,* a magnificent megalithic sepulchre declared a National Monument and set in a meadow landscape typical of Extremadura. Corresponding as it does to a dolmen type structure with a large chamber and a long passage divided into sections, all of which was covered in its day by a large, highly visible at the time, artificial tumulus made of earth and stones.

Scattered remains we know to be from the Bronze and Iron ages have been discovered in Mérida itself, as well as some archaeological sites in the surrounding area. Some objects of which are worthy of significant mention from a cultural point of view, as is the case of the gold rings and ankle supports belonging to what is know as the "Tesoro de Mérida", in the British Museum and classified as Late Bronze Age. Also a curious bronze figurine of what appears to be a Phoenician warrior, also preserved in the British Museum and dated around 700 BC, that is to say, the time the Greeks and Phoenicians imparted their cultural heritage upon the entire southern peninsula.

Another exceptional piece, from a somewhat later period (400-500 BC), is the so called "carritó de Mérida", preserved in the Saint-Germain-en-Laye museum, in Paris, probably of votive origins and a further demonstration of the arrival of eastern Mediterranean influences in the area. Other objects lead to the same conclusion, Kernos, Iberian votives etc. Even so, there isn't actually any reliable evidence of the existence of a pre-Roman fort or settlement. Before the Roman city came to be founded, the territory of which Mérida was a part was located on the frontier or conflict zone

Sharpened stone.

between the Vettones and Turdetanos although it was an area also raided by the warmongering Lusitanian populations. The indigenous population of Roman Mérida had to therefore incorporate aspects appertaining to Turdetanos, Vettones, and Lusitanians.

Dión Casio (155-235 AD), in his *Historia Romana* (53, 25, 2), stated literally: "The war over (that between the Cantabrians and the Asturians) and Augustus discharged the most veteran soldiers, granting them permission to establish a city in Lusitania known as *Augusta Emerita*"

Centuries later, San Isidoro, being of the same opinion, wrote along similar lines in his *Etimologías* (15, 1, 69).

These are the principal texts and main sources of information on the founding of the colony of *Augusta Emerita*. Added to these are other, archaeological documents, which provide answers to certain questions around these early times: its

inhabitants, the delegated authorities during its foundation, the layout of the city, its first monuments, etc.

It has been agreed, in accordance with these sources, that the city had to have been founded in the year 25 BC, following the conclusion of one of attacks during Rome's war against the rebellious Cantabrians and Asturians, resulting in the storming of Lancia. Some authors, nevertheless, prefer to put the date back to the year 19 BC, when the Cantabrian wars effectively reached their final conclusion.

In spite of all this, even though we accept the year 25 BC to be the chronological date when the colony of *Augusta Emerita* was created, it is no less certain that a strategic location such as this, par excellence, to which we have already made reference, couldn't go unnoticed to "Roman eyes" and who had already established *praesidia* (strongholds) throughout the zone: *Metellium* (Medellín), *Norba* (Cáceres), *Scallabis* (Santarem), *Pax Iulia* (Beja), as well as others. It was very strange therefore that this land from where control could easily have been exercised over the main routes, was avoided, above all, by Caesar, the great strategist and topographer.

The military veterans who settled here were deduced to be from the *V Alaudae* and the *X Gemina* legions, according to coins issued from Mérida's mint, although they very probably came also from the XX *Victoria Victrix* legion.

Publio Carisio, a general who had taken part in the wars against Asturias was appointed legate and maxim authority of the foundation, but the factotum, the true master, was to be non other than Marco Vipsanio Agripa, since he was charged with keeping various archaeological documents.

The driving force behind the foundation was that of constructing a stronghold, on a par with tangible evidence of the advantages of Romanisation *(speculum ac propugnaculum imperii romani)*.

The new colony thus became a strategic enclave in the midst of lands which were poorly dominated and somewhat averse in principal to Romanisation. Its strategic value came to be recognised as a favourable place, by the Guadiana pass, over which a bridge was constructed which connected the land, then known as Betica, with the troubled

lands of the north and northwest and which were so important to the Roman exchequer.

The new colony, which inherited a role which was initially played by Medellín, came to be, as a result of the new conquests, the epicentre of Roman politics in the peninsula. *Emerita,* with its extensive territory, also joined forces with other provinces, Tarragona and Betica, with which it formed an important communication centre, a crossroads with the west of the peninsular.

The indigenous population very probably joined up with the veterans and became involved in the new situation, creating as such, a semi-military type population nucleus, as was the case with Estrabón.

Somewhat later, with the city firmly established, it came to be the designated capital of the new province of Lusitania.

If the motives relating to political, military, social and administrative importance were evident at the time the colony was founded, then also were those relating to the area's topography. Mérida's topography has two particular features to be taken into account: the river Guadiana and the hills, though not of an excessive elevation and where the city came to be established.

View of Mérida from an etching by De Laborde.

Augusta Emerita, like many ancient cities, owes its foundation to the river. Mérida was the only place for many kilometres where it was possible to ford the *Ana* with little difficulty. If we add to this, the existence of an island in the middle of the channel, it is not difficult to imagine its significant strategic value.

The importance of road access was vital, as was the control of the roads, which was to be the deciding factor in the location of the new city.

The Roman roads and the city's main streets are prolongations of, or correspond to, one and the same, as is the case in *Emerita,* where the *decumanus maximus* was recognised as the main route from the south to the Castilian plateau known as la Meseta and the *kardo maximus,* which was none other, to a large extent, than the north eastern route.

The island of Guadiana, therefore, together with the shallow depth of the waters which made the river fordable at this point, was the biggest deciding factor when it came to considering the location of *Emerita*. A long bridge was constructed here, according to the width of the channel and which provided free passage across the river.

The chosen site for the location of the city was on the right hand riverbank, which, although it presented some difficulties, was the most suitable. The main problem was the formidable floods caused by the river current, witnessed in ancient times and demonstrated by the bridge's restoration in the time of the Visigoths. To avoid devastation and reinforce the slight elevation offered by the river's bank, the colonisers constructed a strong dyke built of dry-stone with buttresses of ashlars, along the length of the river bank. Thanks to these defences the city, according to ancient sources, was protected from the devastating floods, like Rome and many other cities.

This amazing construction, highly praised by Morena de Vargas and who in his famous work refers to the fact that Felipe II and his architect Juan de Herrera were astounded during their stay in Mérida.

If the difficulties or disadvantages represented by establishing the city on the right bank of the river were minimal and were able to be resolved, the advantages were certainly at a premium.

On the one hand, water was plentiful, not the case on the opposite bank, and the springs discovered within what was the Roman colony enclosure were numerous, various cisterns being constructed to make the most of them, some of which we can still see today. Moreover, from a meticulous study of the terrain, the existence of certain depressions together with various streams and water currents were discovered. Which is how, by making the most of the natural resources on offer, Mérida's three aqueducts came to be created: "Cornalvo" *(Aqua Augusta),* "Rabo de Buey-San Lázaro" and "Proserpina".

The topography of the land also offers a range of hills which served perfectly to establish important installations. On the slopes of the nearby "San Albín", they were able to construct, "Greek style", theatre terraces and part of those of the neighbouring amphitheatre with the resultant advantages.

Finally, the place itself was suitable for defence, the surrounding walls well structured, following the sinuous contours of the hills.

Apart from this, the land around Mérida was and still is good, with excellent cultivation terrain, pastures for livestock as well as rich hunting grounds.

Also well known, as a result of the excellent survey carried out on behalf of the city, by the distinguished don Vicente Sos Baynat, are the areas mineral resources and it could be said that the Romans had every possible resource at their disposition to construct their new city: marbles, granites, diorites, sands, gravels, etc.

The new settlement was endowed with an extensive territory, or municipal district to use a present day though not exactly precise term, which was distributed with a generosity uncommon at the time.

Nevertheless, in spite of the news brought to us by surveyors, valuable if somewhat incomplete, we are still a long way from the whole picture. It is certainly true that the limits of this territorial district can be more or less convincingly established, but it is no less certain that we know little in relation to the structure of the colonial *ager,* the division of land, its viability, demography, etc.

We can also affirm that this territorial extension, of almost 20,000 km² was divided into three prefectures or administrative districts. Their boundaries were, to the north, the territory of *Norba;* to the south, the *conventus bispalensis* and *cordubensis;* to the east, Valdecaballeros and to the west, the region of Borba, Estremoz, with its marble quarries.

Within this territory, with its excellent cultivation land, pastures, an abundance of mineral reserves and quarries, its viability well defined by the Roman roads which united the various nuclei of the same, there was a thriving economy throughout the Roman period, which marked the progress of the *colonia Augusta Emerita.*

Although it is true that we know, up to certain point, some of the determining factors which influenced the founding of the colony, they are no more than those which have been dispelled in relation to the course of its history.

We have to suppose that the city of Augusta, likewise Hispania, received an almighty boost with the advent of the Flavius dynasty, a boost which couldn't have been a long way off the former arrival, in the time of the emperor Otón, of a new population contingent, this time of purely Italian origin, which brought new blood to the perhaps only partially populated city and which was soon to reach the considerable figure of 25,000 inhabitants.

Being a communications nucleus (with up to nine principal routes from the city providing a link with the Empire's main cities), it was also a point of reference on the later named "Viá de la Plata", *(iter ab Emerita Asturicam),* which connected Seville and the Atlantic with the semi-Romanized lands of the north; the city experienced significant commercial and industrial economic development, converting it, together with its role as administrative capital of the extensive Lusitanian province, into a political administration centre of the first order. With the protection and help procured by the provincial governor and a comprehensive bureaucratic mechanism, a cultural life and the demand for basic necessities developed which soon attracted the Empire's principal artists and artisans, who created some of

Roman road, in the Museum grounds.

𝔐

their best works in this city, some of which can be seen in the halls of Mérida's Museum.

We have no information on the city's repercussions during the much talked about "crisis" in the 3rd century and neither does archaeological evidence show any indications to this effect. On the contrary, there are, from the beginnings of the 4th century enough testimonies to indicate the city's economic recovery with the advent of the Constantinople dynasty. Epigraphic monuments from this time speak of the reconstruction of the most important public buildings: the theatre and the circus, dilapidated by the passing of time *(vetustate conlapsum)* as well as new places,

thanks to the munificence of Constantine and his sons, supervised by the governor over the entire *dioceses Hispaniarum* who, from the last administrative reform, resided in Mérida.

A few years earlier the city had the doubtful honour of appearing in the chronicles for the Santa Eulalia martyrdom (in the year 303), an active member of the doubtless very numerous and problematic Christian community, with its hierarchical organisation, at least from the time of the persecution of Decio (3rd century), in which the bishop Marcial renounced his title, accused of libel.

Following Milan's freedom of worship edict (313), Mérida, along with Seville and Tarragona became one of the three Spanish cities to have been endowed with metropolitan ranking. Indeed, the Archbishop of Mérida extended his jurisdiction over 12 Episcopal seats and this power, not only spiritual, was an extremely important stimulus with regard to the urban development of the city, which soared to one of the highest positions on the scale of the Empire's major cities, as proclaimed by poet Marco Ausonio (second half of the 4th C) in his *ordo nobelium urbium,* and which put Mérida in ninth position of the 17 most important cities in the Empire.

Once the initial invasions of the towns to the north were underway Mérida and Lusitania, in general, were battlefields between the Suevi the Alani and the Vandals, who wanted to occupy by the strength of arms, the void left by the disappearance of imperial authority.

We know from sources that, around 409, the Alani occupied Lusitania, later joining forces with the Vandals, who settled in Betica, and that

Visigoth coin.

━━━━━━━━━━━━━ ℳ ━━━━━━━━━━━━━

together they fought the Suevi, close to Mérida, defeating them completely, their king perished by drowning in the Guadiana. Shortly after, the Vandals having left for Africa, Rechila the Suevic once again occupied Mérida after defeating the imperial army in 442, making the city his capital, his power having been reinforced by defeating the Visigoths (457) who had attempted to recover the city for the Roman government.

With imperial authority disappeared completely, the Visigoths seized the city in 469, which then came to be the capital of one of the six provinces which together formed Hispania, the governing doge residing here and even during the reign of Agila, it came to acquire the status of capital of the kingdom which subsequently, for political reasons, was advised to be transferred to Toledo.

During the rebellion by Hermenegildo against his father, the Roman-Hispano substrate and the opinion of Mérida's metropolitan dwellers, authentic bastions of orthodoxy, heavily favoured the rebel when it came to make a decision, since the city had endured severe confrontations with the royal army and reprisals from civil power against the head of the Catholic clergy, Masona, and who became widely recognised after Recaredo was converted.

From a short work from the 7th century, *De vita et míraculis Patrum Emeritensium,* attributed to deacon Paulo, we know of the city's flourishing economic and commercial activities in this time, for the most part endorsed by its archbishops, authentic substitutes for civil power, who constructed schools and hospitals with the same enthusiasm as monasteries and basilicas and also made funds available to set up loan companies, which lent money at low interest rates to the most needy classes. Architectural remains found to date, are eloquent proof of the flourishing art and culture and which have impressed upon more than one erudite, perhaps excessively, that Mérida was the birthplace of Visigoth art.

It is believed that, following the defeat of Guadalete (711) the remainder of the defeated Visigoth army, led by don Rodrigo, took refuge in Mérida, upholding a long siege which lasted for more than a year, after which and following a pact made with the victorious Muza, the city was occupied without causing any destruction and the people allowed to maintain their civil rights and traditions.

Although at first the conquest was accepted without too much disapproval by the people who were tired of internecine struggles by Gothic nobles, in a short time the strong influx of the Hispano-Visigoth population was an incessant breeding ground for rebellions and conspiracies against the Caliph power, in which Muladies and Mozarabs from Mérida participated jointly, up to the point that Abderramán II, tired of such turbulent dwellers, ordered its walls to be knocked down (834) and the district closest to the bridge and which guarded the entrance to the bridge to be demolished, and to construct a fort which would serve this purpose and protect the garrison in the event of any of the frequent disturbances caused by its restless inhabitants.

Without any doubt, so much instability provoked a mass exodus of the population and a considerable loss of the city's influence, to such a degree that, following the disappearance of the Omeya caliphate, the capital status of the kingdom of "Taifa" came to be established in the neighbouring Badajoz. However, all those years of skirmishes, ransacking and pillaging did nothing to erase the city's splendid past, and even in the 9th century Rasis the Moor wrote: "I swear to you there is not a man in this world who can adequately praise the marvels of Mérida".

If, as local historians have confirmed, the Arab period was detrimental to Mérida, the Christian Reconquest of Spain couldn't have had a worse start for the ancient capital. Mérida's first historic opportunity to recuperate its lost glory was dispelled when the city, after being conquered by the Christian armies, under the command of Alfonso IX of León (10th January 1230), came to be under the servitude of the Archbishop of Santiago, who had transferred the Archbishop of Mérida to Santiago by special dispensation from Calixto II (26th February 1120), at the request of Alfonso VII. To make matters worse, Archbishop Gelmírez, fearful of the resurgence of Mérida and the return of its former privileges, a few years later, reserving his ecclesiastical jurisdiction, surrendered the dominion of Mérida to the Order of Santiago, in exchange for property belonging to the latter in Galicia and it was under this jurisdiction that the city remained until the states became incorporated with the Crown.

Following various failed attempts to recuperate its metropolitan seat, Mérida, for a lengthy period of time, came to be a simple town devoid of any historical importance, though still set in a strategic location, at the crossroads of all the king's highways and dumb witness to all the travellers journeying from north to south and from east to west, until the first indications of economic recovery appeared in the time of the Catholic Kings, eloquent proof of which are the constructions, both civil and ecclesiastical with which the city became embellished (municipal council, Corbos and Roca palaces, parish church of Santa Eulalia, Santa María, etcetera).

Once again, down to its strategic position, as was the case in former times, on the event of the wars with Portugal (Juan I, 1382 and Juan II, 1430), the district of Mérida became, much to its regret, the scene of bloody skirmishes between the supporters of Isabel and those of Juana *la Beltraneja*. It is precisely in the area surrounding the city, more specifically, the Albuera stream, where a decisive battle took place in which the conflict practically favoured Isabel and Fernando, and in which the master of Santiago, don Alonso de Cárdenas was notably courageous. However, this still did not prevent the city remaining for some time in the hands of the warmongering Countess of Medellín, doña Beatriz Pacheco. Once the peace treaty was signed, the city underwent an extensive reconstruction and decoration programme to the benefit of not only the palaces and churches but also the roman bridge, which due to its strategic position, had been the target of attacks from one side or another.

During the reign of the first Hapsburgs the city was forced to continue its slow and somewhat unremarkable restoration process, without hardly any news of interest and any there was, purely anecdotal. There exists no documentary evidence of whether the municipality of Mérida took part in the war of the communities, and only a single piece of news mentions the passing of King Carlos I (1526) on his way to Seville, where he was to marry Isabel of Portugal.

In 1557 the city prepared itself, with all due solemnity, to house the remains of the emperor's sister, Leonora of Austria, queen of Portugal and France, who passed away in Talavera and was buried in the church of Santa María, until later being transferred to El Escorial in 1574. Some years later, in 1580, it was Felipe II who passed some days in Mérida whilst preparing the annexation of Portugal. As long ago as 1619 the chronicles mentioned, with special delight, the city's visit by King Felipe III, on the 4th May, en his way to Portugal, along with the public festivities dedicated to such illustrious visitors.

If we adopt the opinion of the local erudite don Vicente Navarro de Castillo, with reference to the fact that the early Hapsburgs' reign was a time of social and economic strength for Mérida, we also have to consider that, the reign of Felipe IV was, by contrast, mournful and disastrous for the city. Indeed, the Portuguese and Catalonian uprisings brought grave repercussions to the district of Mérida. The city's close proximity to Portugal, in particular, converted Mérida's lands into an infinite source of men, provisions and money, in an attempt to suffocate the rebellion which lasted for twenty long years and which eventually caused the people to withdraw, fleeing in the face of levies, compulsory lodgings and appropriations. It comes as no surprise that at the end of the conflict (1668) travellers at that time referred to the city in no other words than those of devastated, poor and abandoned.

Neither did the inauguration of the Bourbon dynasty bring about an improvement in the

Iron bridge.

standard of living for the people of Mérida. Once Felipe V (1700) was proclaimed, giving rise to the Spanish War of Succession, from which Mérida's lands were fairly distant, until in 1704, an Anglo-Dutch army disembarked in Portugal intent on invading Spain by the borders of Extremadura. From that time and up until 1709, the calamitous scenes of the former century were to be repeated, the district of Mérida once again the setting for combats, skirmishes, and pillaging from opposing forces, with the resulting damage to an already declining economy which still hadn't recovered from the demise of the former century.

From the reigns of Carlos III and Carlos IV, the chronicles bring us news of the queen of Portugal's brief spell in the city in 1796, en route for Madrid, where she was to have a meeting with King Carlos III, and that of Carlos IV and his wife, on the way to Badajoz, where they spent some days in the company of Godoy, the royal adviser. What is more, the learned thinking of the time, personified by the

Count of Campomanes, signified the resurgence of the city's agricultural activities, a tendency prevailing throughout the country, only to be violently dashed a few years later by the War of Independence.

Indeed, Mérida, like almost every Hispanic municipality, was unable to save itself from the ravages of war. In 1809, on the 31st of March, Marshall Victor's troops entered Mérida without meeting with any resistance, shortly to abandon the city, after having ransacked the wheat supplies and the Santa Eulalia church and not returning until 1810. However, it was in 1811 when an authentic artillery battle was fought from inside the city against the invading troops posted in the surrounding area, the outcome of which was the destruction of more than 25 percent of the city's hamlets and the population fleeing en mass to the country. In 1812 the city, or what was left of it, was silent witness to the French troops withdrawal, which didn't prevent them from carrying out some archaeological pillaging of which the chronicles still remind us today.

During the reign of Fernando VII (1823) Mérida once again received a contingent of French troops, this time sent by the king himself, and which was marching to Seville to impose the absolute power of the sovereign.

Once this entire fearsome era came to an end and the district of Mérida no longer the scene of forthcoming civil conflicts, a period of slow economic growth was initiated, being a definitive boost, added to which was the construction of the railway (1862) which translated into the simultaneous demographic increase and consistent expansion of the city centre which was to continue for a third of the century. Mérida's slow but progressive revival, only interrupted by our last civil conflict and the consequential post war hardships, was seen to be rising as a result of the strong development in the fifties, during which the city, in addition to its specific influence as a communications nucleus became steadily transformed into an industrial and services city. Added to this was the initiation, in the second decade of the century, of the systematic excavations of the city's historical buildings and monuments; almost uninterrupted to this day, the valuation of the monuments and the promotion of its archaeological heritage, today overseen by the Council of Extramadura, the city being declared by Royal Decree, on the 8th February 1973, as a Conjunto Histórico Arqueológico, the creation of the Museo Nacional de Arte Romano, inaugurated by their Royal Highnesses the King and Queen of Spain, on the 19th September 1986, and the declaration by UNESCO, on the 8th December 1993, of Mérida's archaeological buildings and monuments as a World Heritage Site, all of which have transformed this city into an appealing tourist nucleus of prime importance, attracting hundreds of thousands of visitors each year.

Lastly, the city being designated an autonomous capital, headquarters of the autonomous government and Regional Parliament has transformed Mérida into an administrative centre and public services city, restoring it to the former glory usurped for fifteen centuries. Nowadays the city, with close to 60,000 inhabitants, together with a first class hotel and tourist infrastructure and an extensive network of facilities, has wisely combined the past with the present and confronts the future with hope, enthusiasm and optimism, aware of both its glorious past and its brilliant future.

Mérida town hall.

··· PRE-ROMAN MÉRIDA ···

Observing the tremendous urban task undertaken by the Romans, we shouldn't be too surprised that to find the most significant documents relating to the construction of Pre-Roman towns on Mérida's land, we have to distance ourselves from the city's boundaries. For this reason, we would like to propose a visit to the Dolmen de Lácara, the pictorial landscape of the Calderita and that of the sierra of Arroyo de San Serván.

𝔐

Dolmen de Lácara.

THE MEGALITHIC SEPULCHRE OF LÁCARA

The megalithic sepulchre of Lácara, declared since 1931 to be a National Monument, is one of the most spectacular monuments in the region of Extremadura and an excellent exponent of megalithic architecture from the west of the peninsula. Corresponding to the denominated type with a long passage and circular chamber, it is possible to appreciate the three elements which define these funereal monuments: a circular burial chamber 5,10 metres in diameter, a passage almost

20 metres long divided into three sections and covering the entire structure, an earth and stone covered burial mound, 3,5 metres high of an elliptical form which extends up to 35 metres at its longest point.

The construction is of large blocks of set stone, higher in the burial chamber than the passage, covered by huge flat slabs creating an irregular roof with lintels. Its purpose was a burial site, that is to say, destined to house collective burials, accompanied by some simple items: ceramic vases, stone tools, adornments, metal objects, etc. The objects uncovered in the Almago Basch excavations, now in the Museum at Badajoz, do in fact reveal how the sepulchre was reutilized during the Bronze Age for identical funeral purposes.

To reach this site, it is necessary to take the N-630 road, and the minor road which leads from this to Nava de Santiago, once past the town of Aljucén, the site is signposted a few kilometres away.

LA CALDERITA CAVE

La Calderita cave is an illustration of the main features of simple cave paintings found in the south of the peninsular, with various large simple outline shapes created from red coloured plant dyes. Particularly interesting are the representations of idols and anthropomorphs with suggestions of eyes, forelimbs, etc., which don't appear to form scenes but rather they reflect expressive stereotypes of some unknown content, the depiction of which is comparable with the idols and decorative ceramics of Chalcolithic times. As is the case in almost all the pictorial sites, the place itself overlooks a hilly expanse alongside erosive plains.

Located as it is in the sierra de Peñas Blancas, between the villages of Alange and la Zarza, the site is accessed by the minor road which provides a link between Mérida and these two populations.

THE SAN SERVÁN CAVE PAINTINGS

The San Serván cave painting collection includes more than thirty pictorial sites spread throughout the sierra, with a great variety of images, many of

Simple painting in the Calderita cave complex.

which include anthropomorphs, idols, quadrupeds, suns, rods and what could possibly be a cart, an interesting image, since it denotes a later chronology, reinforcing the durability of these artistic manifestations: Chalcolithic, Bronze Age and the beginning of the Iron Age.

Of the anthropomorphs, the most eloquent are those with asafoetida forelimbs; and also the swallows, the silhouettes of which are very much like this bird; the bi-triangular etc. Among the idols, those which have eyes and the quadrupeds are usually interpreted to be canines, sheep and at times deer recognizable by what appears to be antlers.

The sites are distributed throughout the sierra de San Serván; reached by taking the National A5 road, turning off onto the minor road leading to the town of Arroya de San Serván.

··· ROMAN MÉRIDA ···

TOPOGRAPHY AND CITY PLAN OF ROMAN MÉRIDA

Present day investigations into Mérida's town distribution layout constitutes the unknown factors which have arisen from finding the present day city literally on top of the ancient one, a most appealing undertaking, faced as it is with this archaeological site, the labours of which are recompensed by the constant discovery of new facts which turn up in excavations in the city.

The present state of our knowledge leads us to believe that the *colonia Augusta Emerita* was created *ex novo,* that is to say, on land which at the time was not occupied by a significant population nucleus, although it is probable that there could have existed a small castellum, the role of which was to control and keep watch over the river

Bronze coin with a pair of bulls and a priest outlining the original enclosure.

M

intersection, in a place which was frankly fordable and surrounded two rivers, the *Ana* and the *Barraeca,* and which was a factor in the towns defence attributes.

Later, in the founding period, the ford, being the determining factor in the location of the city since it facilitated the construction of a large bridge which, in addition to establishing the territory's layout, defined for the best part, the urban route, since one of the new town's main thoroughfares, the

decumanus maximus, albeit with a slight curve, followed the line of the road to the bridge.

Up to the present time, two fundamental theories have been formulated on what was believed to be the urban district. One of them, supported by various archaeologists from the first half of the 20th century, amongst which was German archaeologist Schulten, who explained that the colony initially covered an area, including the boundaries which extended towards the *decumanus maximus,* between the Puerta de la Villa or town gates, and the Puerta del Puente, the bridge gates, and between the "Arco de Trajano" and a hypothetical "Arco de Cimbrón", in the direction of the *kardo maximus.* The other theory, equally devised at this time, principally by the English archaeologist, Richmond, who believed that the colonial area practically covered the city nucleus from the beginning, leaving spaces "empty" which, as was the case with other well known cities, would be occupied when the needs derived from the city's boom arose.

Serious drawbacks make us discard the first of the theories, whilst the second seems closer to reality, although it still requires some clarification.

Augusta Emerita would therefore have been an example more in keeping with the framework of town planning ideas from the time of Augustus, than conceived to be a "large scale" long term plan from the start.

The walled city

Significant vestiges of Mérida's wall have been conserved in certain sections and the excavations made in recent years, since the seventies, have provided information which has enabled us to draw a more accurate picture. This fieldwork has, similarly established the walls chronology, which falls right on the colony's early years, at the time of the principality of Augusto, although with some possible modifications to its layout and subsequent alterations, such as those corresponding to a later period, possible in the 5th century AD, when the wall, at least on the river side was reinforced by another strong wall, this time constructed of granite ashlars, with rectangular shaped towers of the same material.

The structure of Mérida's city wall, which can be seen in the grounds to the "Casa del Anfiteatro" as well in the Alcazaba, displays a central core of earth and stone with well aligned facings to both sides in local stone (diorite). Every so often, the monotony of the wall has been broken with semicircular towers of the same morphology as the wall itself.

Thanks to the description from 17th century chronicler, Moreno de Vargas, it has been possible to reconstruct the perimeter of the Roman city, which corresponds to the layout as it was in the 18th and 19th centuries, before urban expansion. The city plan, due to topographical factors, was of a trapezoidal outline.

Of the walled area it has only been possible at the present time to uncover one gateway, located as it was at the entrance to the bridge, in the Alcazaba area, the details of which on account of their significance will be explained accordingly. Similar gateways must have been located at the opposite end of the *decumanus,* the "Puerta de la Villa", or town gates, the part remains of which were recently made visible, also at the ends of the *kardo,* at the Cerro de "El Calvario" and in the vicinity of the present day Plaza de Toros. In addition to these are others, though smaller, such as those discovered in the archaeological site at Morerías, in the grounds of the Amphitheatre and next to the existing gateway, from a later period, in the calle del Arzobispo Massona.

Decumanus maximus.

— ℳ —

Over time, the colonial boundary came to be overflowing and new districts were established outside the city, alongside the roads leaving the city and next to the necropolis areas. This "districts", made up of houses and industrial buildings, which alternated with the aforementioned burial grounds, can be seen in the grounds of the Museum and the "Casa del Mitreo", amongst other places.

We know some of the details of the city's water mains, although the restoration proposed at the start of the century is no longer fully acceptable. According to the plan, published at that time by archaeologist Maximiliano Macías, fourteen drains were orientated at right angles to the river, whereas nine were parallel to the current. Only one, corresponding to the *kardo maximus,* drained into the Albarregas river, although it is probable that this wasn't the only one. Conveniently other researchers have recently clarified the observations made by this distinguished archaeologist from Mérida. Uniformity presided over the construction of these sanitary drains, the outlets of which can be seen at the site of the dam on the Guadiana river.

As far as it is possible to make out, the streets were of a more or less regular grid layout, which demarcated *insulae* or housing blocks of 100-110 metres in length by 50-60 metres wide, although some are shorter, being 80 metres by 70-75 metres.

Of the urban structure, despite the difficulties involved in its research, the layout of various *viae* or roads are well known, above all those of *decumanus* and *kardu,* those found in the Arab

Temple on calle Holguín.

— ℳ —

Alcazaba quarter and Amphitheatre, as well as others now no longer apparent. All appear to have been paved with great flagstones of bluish diorite, which came from the quarry of the neighbouring town of La Garrovilla.

One special feature of Mérida's streets is the arrangement of arcades along the most important. These arcades, similar to our present day version, were likewise supported by granite pillars.

Of the city's public areas, we know something of the forums, equally the one denominated colonial as the provincial, which are illustrated on site.

Another well defined quarter within the colonial city district was the location of the entertainment buildings, the Theatre and the Amphitheatre, inaugurated in the colony's early years, to be later extended and reformed, and also the Circus, now in the first part of the 1st century AD, the ruins of which have been well preserved and are described elsewhere in this guide.

Likewise, we can say the same of the houses, of Mediterranean design.

The necropolis or burial sites were arranged around the city, next to the roads, by way of a "funeral crown". In the different areas of those which can be defined, the sepulchres are seen to be perfectly aligned and of an almost urban structure. The typology of the burial sites is comprehensive and diverse.

The most important necropolis sites are to be found at the exit to the bridge over the Guadiana, with quadrangular mausoleums from the from the 1st and 2nd centuries AD, located in the Albarregas valley and in the vicinity of the Theatre, the one known as the oriental necropolis, which extends as far as the Circus and which can be considered the most spectacular of the structures preserved.

During the Visigoth period, Mérida's city centre didn't undergo any significant changes, although the public areas were significantly modified with new buildings. Two areas of the city were particularly well presented: one, that of the present day Plaza de España, where, probably on the same site as the Santa María church, was the *ecclesia semior* or former cathedral, and the other, that of the Santa Eulalia church, where, under the protection of the basilica, it was discovered some years ago to be a religious complex of the first order.

Similarly various districts were created in the outskirts, around the basilicas.

The Bridge Gateway

We know of various gateways within the walled city of Mérida, but none quite as impressive as the one which provides access to the city via the Puente or bridge.

Significant remains of this gateway came to be found during excavations carried out towards the end of the seventies, even though it was reduced to the foundations.

It was a *porta gemina,* that is to say, with twin portals, of similar dimensions, one presumably the entrance and the other the city's exit, each flanked by somewhat higher quarter circle towers, initially with corner spur stones to properly guide the uncommon traffic which for this reason passed through, denoted by diverse reforms, perceptible equally on the road's two levels, as the access itself.

The gateway was closed by means of a portcullis *(cataracta),* the mechanism to which can still be seen in the entrance portal and on the gates, apparently of wood. The interiors are both in the form of vaulted passages.

Strange though it may seem at first to see that the gates are not exactly perpendicular to the bridge, but as demonstrated by other examples from the Roman world, this is due to, amongst other reasons, the structural role played by the bridge.

From its design, it appears to correspond to those displayed on coins from the colonial mint, from the time of Augustus, which if this is the case would be relatively easy to reconstruct its elevation.

Morerías archaeological site.

Its destruction was mainly due to the redistribution of space during the construction of the Alcazaba, the gateway being converted into a defence bulwark to protect the bridge.

The Morerías archeological site

The expropriation of land on calle Morerías towards the end of the 80's, by the Junta de Extremadura, for the construction of a building designed to house the Presidencia de la Junta, the local governing body and four other Consejerías or departments (at the hands of the prestigious architect Juan Navarro Baldeweg), made it possible to excavate a site of more than 12,000 m², which has provided valuable evidence with regard to the city's historical evolution and urban development from the time of the Romans up until the present day, with clearly stratified Roman, Visigoth, Islamic, medieval, modern and contemporary periods. What is more, it has enabled, in a rather singular manner to evaluate various city structures, (the wall, roads, gateways, sewage system, housing blocks, houses, baths, etc.) observing the changes of use that these, immersed within the city's logical evolutionary process, have gradually undergone throughout a prolonged chronological period.

The wall is without doubt the most monumental feature of the "Morerías" site. Lining the entire western façade of the site, parallel to the river and extending for almost two hundred metres. The conservation of the wall is somewhat mediocre, although in some sections it reaches the far from insignificant height of four metres, and in which some of the most distinctive features of the original wall from the founding period are still recognisable: well presented *opus incertum* facings to the outside, with mortar on the inside. It has been possible to document up to four small gates or minor accesses, two metres wide, and a rectangular tower, probably to defend one of the gateways, partially preserved and incorporated within a wall from a later period, possibly at some time during the 5th century AD, to confront the continuous wave of attacks from invaders, a time when a good part of it was strongly reinforced with granite ashlars, almost doubling the thickness of the original wall.

The space between the wall and the nearby river dyke was taken up by another necropolis site, initially Roman, which survived until the late medieval period.

A road network which cut through the land with definitive regularity is testimony to the precision of Roman urbanisation, with housing blocks sloping steeply down to the river, achieved by a basic skimming technique on the natural rock to provide a route for the main roads, in this case *kardo minor* which cuts through the land from north to south, crossed perpendicularly by *decumani* which led to the exit gateways in the direction of the river. The robust roads were paved in hard diorite in shades of black and blue as well as some quartzite slabs, all of which included a good drainage system below with walled sewers and stone built vaults. The dignified streets, some of which had arcades sections supported by granite columns, for the benefit of pedestrians, above all those on the approach to the provincial district forum, which in much later times

didn't actually prevent them from deteriorating, as was the case even in private houses, evidence of the decadence in municipal administration in those uncertain times.

It has been possible to demarcate up to six sizeable blocks 83 m long by 34 m wide, in which there would have been up to thirteen large homes, of a rectangular design which, as was the norm in *domus* houses, were arranged around a central patio. Some of them were later to be re-created by the addition of a second floor, tiling the patios and fitting sumptuous private baths, for which it was also necessary to construct cisterns. The majority also included commercial premises, workshops or shops, next to each other on the same façade or adjacent corners.

The most spectacular of all of these is the popularly dubbed "Casa de los Mármoles", meaning the marble house, which occupies an entire block, its western façade adjacent to the wall. The eastern side is next to *kardo,* to the north, one of the ancient gateways and to the south, *decumanus,* the road which leads to a small gateway in the wall. Considered as it is, to be a large *domus* furnished with sumptuous ornamental decor, by means of a carefully selected combination of white marble and black slate, which enhanced its layout, around the flamboyantly paved central patio. It also has *cubicula* paths, numerous rooms with apses and private baths.

Silent testimony to the instability to which Hispania was submitted, following the 5th century invasions were the ashlar reinforcements which in some places doubled the thickness of the original wall, and the Visigoth constructions, superimposed over the ancient Roman quarter with no respect for urban layout, equally to be destroyed after a long siege which ended with the city being conquered by the Muslims in the year 713. These latest conquerors, however, didn't return to occupy the city until well into the 9th century, when there was documented to be as many as six large buildings of a regular design, the majority with a single or triple nave, of Byzantine design, no doubt imported by the Omeya people themselves, relating to the administration of the new Emirate power. After the city was conquered by the troops from León in 1230, this district was cordoned off and left almost

Morerías site.

abandoned, to the remaining Muslim population, being granted the name by which it is known today "La Morería".

Since 2003, together with the evaluation of the site, the Proyecto Alba Plata has undertaken the construction of the *Centro de Interpretación de la Vía de la Plata en Extremadura,* which basically consists of an exhibition of the Roman Road known as the Vía de la Plata and its route through Extremadura. The exhibition expounds upon the road's design and the elements from which it is constructed, as well as its history and value as a cultural link within the region.

The VII Sillas study centre

The discoveries which are continuously being unearthed on the site of what was the *colonia Augusta Emerita* have instigated the creation of a series of tourist enclaves able to furnish the visitor with immediate explanations, whether in the middle of the street, or certain areas of the Roman city, and which have been proposed by various interpretation centres, such that of "Las VII Sillas", meaning the seven seats, named as it is, on account of its proximity to the Theatre.

The name refers to a legend relating to the unusual theatre building, in which, prior to carrying out the excavation of the site, seven large concrete remains were visible which corresponded to the *summa cavea,* individualized after the access gateways to the same were to disappear and which popular imagination considered to be the seats of many other Moorish kings who were brought together here to decide the destinies of *Marida.*

In the Centro de Interpretación visitors can admire the ruins of a *domus* or Roman house, which in its day was of sizeable dimensions and which today is reduced to a couple of rooms, one, not visible, where there appeared the magnificent "Neolithic Mosaic", with a representation of a poet, muses, stations of the cross, victories and scenes from the Nile with pygmies as the protagonists, from whence comes the name of the mosaic, now exhibited in the Museo Nacional de Arte Romano, and another which can be seen on site, an ornamental mosaic from the same date, the middle of the 2nd century AD.

The house was built next to the city walls, verified by a stretch of the wall itself, which can also be seen.

Tourist information is available in the Centre run by the Ayuntamiento de Mérida, the local town council.

BUILDINGS FOR PUBLIC SPECTACULARS: THEATRE, AMPHITHEATRE AND CIRCUS

The Theatre

The Theatre is the most important Roman monument to be preserved in Mérida. Theatre and Amphitheatre were designed by the Romans to be a joint project, selecting various *insulae* or blocks for its installation, in the northwest corner of the city, which turned out to be the most elevated. To avoid the force of the winds, which would bother the spectators and actors, the terraces were set on the hillside slopes of San Albín.

The two public buildings are separate, but at the same time connected, by a road, the same we have to take to begin our tour of the monument. Whilst walking along the aforementioned road we will stop to admire the solidity and reciedumbre of the Theatre's exterior façade constructed with the hardest limestone mortar with square set granite ashlar facings with the typical bevelled edges.

To access the interior of the Theatre we can enter by any one of the 16 doors to the façade, but preferably by those which lead us to the middle terraces, where if we so wish, comfortably seated, we can take a moment or two to study the splendour and magnificence of this unique monument.

The terraces, accessed by vaulted passages *(vomitoria),* were divided into three sections, *(ima, media, and summa cavea),* separated by wide aisles *(praecintiones)* and low walls *(baltei),* which corresponded to the fiercely hierarchical levels of Roman society.

The *summa cavea* or high terrace is the most deteriorated. The vaulted access passages, on having collapsed, became incorporated within the seven large concrete remains, which gave rise to the legend of the "Siete Sillas", or seven seats, the name by which this place is commonly known. It

Roman Theatre ashlars and the results of pillaging.

is this place which was reserved for the slaves and less favoured classes.

The *media cavae,* comprised five rows of terraces which welcomed the free working classes.

The *ima cavea* or lower terrace, consisted of 22 rows of terraces and was reserved for the *equites* or noblemen, according to an inscription (E X D) which, inscribed in one of the steps, is interpreted as *equites decem decreto*

and now reconstructed in brick, were movable seats (subsellia) an occurrence between the years 16 and 15 BC, which perhaps coincides with Mérida's provincial capital status.

At the ends of the semicircle, above the aforementioned passages, were privileged boxes *(tribunalia)* similar to VIP boxes in our present day theatres.

Between the orchestra and the stage *(pulpitum)* runs the proscenium *(proscaeniam),*

The Roman Theatre's terraces.

(decurionum), being, "seating for ten noblemen by decree of the Decurions". Thanks to this inscription, and by making a simple estimation, the capacity of the theatre amounted to some 6,000 seated spectators.

The different areas of the *cavea* are connected by stairs which also served to divide the terraces vertically into sections or *cunei.*

The most preferential place in the Theatre was the *orchestra,* a semicircular area, paved in blue and white marble and reserved for the choir. Placed here, over three levels, originally in marble

an unusual wall which alternates semicircular and rectangular doors in an attempt to improve, if possible, the already perfect acoustics. Small staircases either side connect this to the stage, a place for actors to wander freely, being 60 metres long and 7 metres wide. The stage floor, originally in wood, was protected by a canopy which also served an acoustic role.

The Consecrated Stage of Mérida's Roman Theatre.

The front of the stage *(scaenae frons)* is the most outstanding feature of the building, with three doors, one in the centre *(valva regia),* of a larger size than the two side doors *(valvae hospitalia),* through which the actors would burst onto stage. This splendid "backdrop" consists of a high podium 2.60 metres high, the base for two sections of Corinthian columns which with their respective bases rose to a height of almost 13 metres.

In between the columns were statues of heroic emperors in military vestments, or deified sculptures such as those of gods from the classic pantheon: Ceres, Pluto and Proserpina.

If we enter any one of the stage entrance doors we immediately come across the *choragia* or actors dressing rooms, with marble covered bench seats running the length of the walls.

In prominent theatres, such as this one in Mérida, there would usually be, to the rear, a peristilo surrounded by a portico, where the spectators would stroll between performances. The garden, the appearance of which would not be much different to the one seen today, had a canal, by way of a reservoir, and was profusely decorated with sculptures.

At the very heart of the peristilo, centred by the royal crest, there is a little room paved with marbles where in the course of the archaeological excavations an important collection of sculptures was discovered, the most outstanding of which include the shrouded head of Augustus as high priest, the effigies of Tiberius and Druze and various inscribed monuments which reliably informs us that the place was intentionally designed to pay homage to the emperor.

The Theatre underwent restoration between the years 333 and 335 AD, with the introduction of new decorative architectural elements and the construction of a road which went around the historical building.

Years later, when the theatre lost its naturalization papers, an individual was allowed to construct, within the site itself, his own home, some of the remains of which are still to be seen. Of the accommodation, there is an interesting room with a double apse, which has led excavators to believe that it was the place where the first Christian worship took place in Emerita, baptized with the name of "Casa Basílica", the name by which it is known in archaeological circles. It is, nevertheless, classed as a simple and typically domestic construction from late imperial times. The figures painted on its walls, formerly identified as Christian priests, are representations of the house's servants, a theme which was very much in vogue in late Antiquity. Visible to the left of this noble room and the garden before it are the master of the house's private thermal baths.

The Theatre became buried in modern times, its terraces used to cultivate cereals and vegetables until, at the beginning of the present century, archaeological excavations were initiated, led by don José Ramon Mélida and guided by don Maximiliano Macías, native of Mérida. The restoration work as it is seen today was carried out in the seventies by architect don José Menéndez Pidal. Performances take place in the Theatre every year during the summer season.

ℳ

Below, "Casa Basílica". On the following double page. Scenic view of the front of the Theatre.

The Amphitheatre

The Amphitheatre was built next to the Theatre, making the most of the hillside slopes of San Albín as an aid to the terraces. To make room for its construction, two *insulae* or housing blocks were set aside, both buildings constituting a substantial part of what was the general urban development scheme for the *colonia Augusta Emerita*.

The *cavea* or terraces, with a capacity for 15,000 spectators, was divided into three different areas. The *ima cavea* or section closest to the arena with a row reserved for the preferential judges seats who presided over the games. The *media* and *summa cavea* accommodated a heterogeneous public, accessed as they were by stairs *(scalaria)*.

Merida's Amphitheatre. Above, the Rostrum; below, general view.

Mérida's Roman Amphitheatre is of considerable dimensions. The ellipse measured more than 126 metres at its longest axis point and 102 by 65 metres wide. The arena itself, according to calculations by its excavator J. R. Mélida measured 54 by 41,5 metres

The building's façade is broken periodically by sixteen doorways at the start of the *vomitorio* or passages which lead to different areas on the terraces.

As was the case with other public entertainment buildings, the highest ranking dignitaries presided over the games in exceptional seats, from where they were able to enjoy the games both in great comfort and with a good view of the games. In addition to this stand, there was another, on the west side, the *editoris tribunal,* reserved for those who funded the games.

Each stand displayed a monumental inscription with identical text: "The Emperor Augustus, son of the Divine Caesar, Pontiff Maxim, eleventh consul,

𝕸

Two views of Mérida's Amphitheatre.

decorated with paintings alluding to the games, part of which are exhibited in the Museo Nacional de Arte Romano.

The gladiators entered the arena by two great corridors, the sides of which opened onto rooms, the purpose of which are yet to be determined. It has been suggested they could have been a place of worship to Nemesis, divine protector of the gladiators and to whom they would put their faith in before leaping into the arena. It has also been speculated that they were places reserved for the gladiators themselves, although the reduced

———————— 𝔐 ————————

Relief depicting gladiators and a painting from Mérida's Amphitheatre.

fourteenth Emperor. The honorific mentions inscribed in these long granite lintels tell us exactly when the amphitheatre was inaugurated (in the year 8 BC).

Subsequently, due to archaeological works carried out by Mérida, the discovery of new inscriptions have made it possible to document other stands or galleries, on the north and south sides, in a structure similar to that of the amphitheatre in Verona.

The Amphitheatre's podium was highly ornate with great marble plaques and a sill of ashlars

dimensions of these rooms negate both options. It seems more likely they were designed to house the wild animals, which would also explain the small side window from which they would have able to feed the animals without risk.

Within the arena a large cruciform shaped pit (*fossa arenaria*) has been excavated which served to store the equipment for the spectacles and the cages for the ferocious animals. The *fossa* was hidden from the eyes of the spectators by a platform supported by wooden pillars. As time went on the

Two paintings from the Amphitheatre.

ℳ

walls of the pit received a layer of hydraulic mortar *(opus signinum)* and was used as a water tank.

The majority of the gladiators who took part in the games were of servile standing, although neither was there a shortage of those which were auctioned *(auctorati),* as was the case of certain veteran soldiers conversant with the use of weapons.

The social status of the gladiators was extremely disparate. The *noxi ad gladium ludi damnati* were those condemned to death at these spectaculars, and couldn't be considered gladiators in the true sense of the meaning since, in spite of the fact they were allowed to be armed, not always the case, the majority knew nothing of either handling a sword nor combat techniques, almost certainly guaranteeing death. This must have been the case with *Cassius Victorinus,* a gladiator from Mérida, who died at the age of 35 years, somewhat unusual for a gladiator, who fought like a *retiarius,* that is to say, provided with a net and brandishing a trident.

The gladiators usually confronted each other bearing different arms and techniques, designed to make the combat more attractive. Thus, the *retiarius* was usually opposed by the heavily armed *secutor.* Curiously the other gladiator documented in Mérida belonged to this rank. *Sperchius,* as he was known, was born in Frigia (Asia Minor) and met his death in *Emerita* at the age of 24.

When a gladiator confronted wild animals, he was given the title of *venator.* The impresarios sought to offer exotic beasts in their spectaculars, the reason for which there was a rapidly flourishing trade in beasts coming from Asia and Africa, veritable fortunes being paid for particular species.

Mérida's Amphitheatre was finally abandoned at what must have been the start of the 5th century AD, when it served as a quarry for the benefit of new building constructions. In moderns times this even included dynamiting the *summa cavea.*

The Circus

To construct the Circus, located as it was, some 400 metres east of the colony's perimeter wall, a site was chosen in the valley next to the San Lázaro aqueduct, well connected by one of the main routes, the road which provided a link between Emerita and *Corduba* (Córdoba) and *Toletum* (Toledo), and with which the northern façade eventually lined up. It was only its enormous proportions (more than 30,000 m²) which led the circus to be removed from the area of the public spectacles.

The years have taken their toll on this famous building, leaving it only a little less than impossible to imagine it in its hour of splendour. That said, it is the best preserved example on the Iberian Peninsula.

Remains of Merida's Circus.

Excavation work initiated back in 1920 is yet to be completed, some questions on the building still remaining unanswered. As a result, in the present state of knowledge, the date of its construction cannot be determined, although there is a tendency to think logically that it has to be of the same period as the Theatre and Amphitheatre clearly dated to the time of Augustus.

The shape of the Circus in Mérida is typical of this type of monument, with two long walls which run parallel to finish at one end in a semi circular form and the other slightly curved. These longest sides served to accommodate the terraces. That to the south was based on natural terrain whilst the one to the north side was set on top of huge concrete vaults. The terrace was preserved until the beginning of the last century, if not entirely intact, but more so than it is today. The French traveller Alejandro de Laborde, to whom we owe an excellent collection of engravings of the city, managed to count up to eleven rows of seats. Now only those in the section closest to the arena are still visible. The terraces were organised into *caveae*, in which 30,000 spectators could be comfortably seated. There were preferential places for the editor or the person who funded the games and for the judges *(tribunal judicam),* who arbitrated the circus events.

The *porta pompae,* from where the solemn procession began, was one of the most colossal, in which there were the twelve *carceres* or garages each housing chariots. The *carceres* in the *circo de Emerita* were made up of four pillars, one to each corner, as in the *circo de Leptis Magna* and surrounded by a wall, the exterior of which would be decorated perhaps with columns or pilasters, such as in Bovillae. Once in the passage, accessed through a wide doorway, the teams passed along the spacious passages to occupy the posts assigned to them by drawing lots. When the arbitrator in charge of the races waved a white ensign *(mappa),* the opening mechanisms to the garages were hoisted to permit the chariots to enter the arena, where the aforementioned races were to take place. The arena in the circus of *Emerita* was truly spectacular, measuring more than 400m by almost 96, which put it amongst the largest in its time. A long wall extending 233 metres, lengthways on, divided the area into two in the form of a central spine, from where comes its name *(spina)*. Of the *spina,* there remains only the concrete foundation and as in other circuses, it would have been decorated with sculptures and obelisks, of which only their footprints remains. Both sides of the *spina* were the finishing lines *(metae)* which the chariots had to go round.

The chariots could be pulled either by two *(bigae)* or four *(cuadrigae)* horses and were driven by charioteers, which were grouped together into sports teams or *factiones,* each one identifiable by a colour; namely, the greens, the whites, the reds and the blues. Some of the charioteers who came to glory in the circus at *Emerita* were well-known through other sources. The extensive sporting career of Lusitanian born Cayo Apuleyo Diocles, the most famous *agitator* or charioteer of all times, must have started here. He retired with a considerable fortune at 42 years of age, after having achieved victory on more than 1,462 occasions.

A tiled surface from the second half of the 4th century AD appeared in Mérida and conserved in the Museum shows us in detail the clothing worn by the charioteers, from the representations of two of them, *Marcianus* and *Paulus,* the first of which is also the central figure in an Italian mosaic. Sporting corselets with leather sashes and wide cingulo to which the bridles were secured which, if needed, were cut with a small knife to avoid being dragged around the arena when the chariot tipped over, which was nothing unusual, considering that, as in the case of the mosaic, they were made almost entirely of wicker. The charioteers' vestments were completed by a metal helmet which protected their heads and a riding crop to egg on the horse team.

The circus of *Emerita* was restored in the 4th century AD. An inscription in marble, originally on the site of the *carceres,* where it was found, and now conserved in the Museo Nacional de Arte Romano, informs us of this fact. Inscribed as it was between October of the year 337 and March-April of 340, stating: "In this flourishing and fortunate century, thanks to the joy and clemency of our lords and emperors Flavius Claudio Constantino and Flavius Julio Constante, always victorious and valiant, Tiberius Flavius Laeto, distinguished gentleman and count, ordered that the Circus, the old one of which had been demolished, was to be reconstructed, surrounded by new ornamentations, inundated with water, the task of which was entrusted to the very excellent gentleman Julio

---

ℳ

Another view of the Circus remains.

Mosaic of Charioteers in the Museo Nacional de Arte Romano.

𝔐

Saturnino, governor of the province of Lusitania, its aspect suitably restored, giving the people of this splendid colony the best possible pleasure".

Attention is drawn, from the reading, to the mention of an inundation of water. Some modern authors believe the circus was transformed into a *naumachia,* that is to say, a place in which to celebrate mock naval battles. Its extensive surface area, however, makes this hypothesis rather difficult. Specific sections of the arena were inundated, creating reservoirs, invoking thoughts of invaluable installation techniques.

Perhaps it was a simple installation with sources already in the enclosure. In any eventually it continues to be an unknown factor.

One aspect which is worth bearing in mind is the date the circus was reconstructed, being so late that it demonstrates the fervour of these, the people of Mérida, for spectacles such as these. Not forgetting, that only a few years before the restoration of this monument, the Church Fathers congregated at the I Concilio de Elvira (310 AD), the council, to condemn some of the games which they considered to be defamatory and four years later, the I Concilio de Arlés condemned the charioteers and forced them to abandon their profession beneath the threat of excommunication. It is important to put these pieces of information into context because the fact is that the circus of *Emerita* continued to be the scene of chariot races at least until the 5th century, according to what can be deduced from the epigraph on an interesting memorial discovered on the site known as "Casa Herrera", of which there are extensive accounts in this book. The memorial is in the form of a sepulchre tombstone of the unknown Sabiniano, a charioteer, who lived to be around 46 years. It infers that Sabiniano was both charioteer and Christian at the same time and that he was buried as such, without renouncing a profession which must have been rewarded by a wealth of fervent admiration, but little in the way of economic benefits. The inscription referring to Sabiniano was posterior to the decree from the Concilio de Elvira, by at least 50 years. If we also take into account that Liberio, the Bishop of Mérida was also in attendance, we can see how the desires of the Church and those of its followers aren't always in line with one another. When the Circus races finally came to be prohibited, a long slow decline began which has been continued until its present reappraisal.

After the first partial restoration was carried out in 1973, which mainly affected the east side section, it wasn't until the nineties when a series of new interventions came into being which have brought considerable advancements with regard to the knowledge of the building, as well as the complete recovery of its base. The most recent proceedings came about in 2001 when the local government body, the Junta de Extremadura, under the auspices of the Proyecto Viá de la Plata, carried out a definitive reassessment of this historical building. The aforementioned proceedings included the consolidation and reintegration of three sectors of the terraces, improving the drainage and access facilities and above all the creation of a Centro de Interpretación, similar to a visitor centre, in which, by means of simple museum archives installations, with audiovisual panels and a model which shows the building as it would have been, in all its former glory, giving us a better understanding of the Roman circus as well as other aspects relative to the spectacle, including its protagonists and the artistic displays around these popular *ludi;* in short, its historical relation with the city and those citizens for whose pleasure it was created.

THE NATIONAL MUSEUM OF ROMAN ART

By way of celebrating Mérida's two thousand years anniversary in 1975, the State decided to create the Museo Nacional de Arte Romano to replace the old Museo Romano, founded by Royal Order on the 26th March 1838, and construct a new building on the site of "Las Torres", in which to preserve and exhibit Mérida's abundant Roman collection, the importance of which has led the museum to be classified as a national institution.

The new museum was inaugurated on the 19th September 1986 by their royal highnesses the King and Queen of Spain, in the presence of the President of the Republic of Italy.

The project is the work of prestigious architect Rafael Moneo Vallés, who has created a magnificent building, justifiably recognised by all and which constitutes a new concept regarding the ethos of Spanish museums. As was the architect's full intention, the building reflects certain aspects of Roman architecture, above all with regard to the design of the crypt, the principal nave and its façades.

The building occupies a plot of some 5,000 m² opposite the Theatre-Amphitheatre complex, the true flagship of Mérida's Roman architecture, to which it is connected by a long tunnel. The entire construction comprises a concrete central structure with brick facings.

Exterior façade of the Museo Nacional de Arte Romano. On the following double page, the inside, over three floors.

A collection from the Forum's Portico, in the Roman Museum.

The building designed by Rafael Moneo to house Méridas collection is magnificent, incorporating a range of flexible features which have been addressed with amazing simplicity by the architect and which, even experts have on occasions have failed to take into account when it comes to undertaking a museum project; the play on light, the opportunity to study the pieces from different angles and perspectives, the clarity of the explanations, the transparency of the display cabinets, etc. This is a building which, in short, will leave nobody feeling indifferent.

The building's western façade, which runs lengthways along the calle de José Ramón Mélida, is hard and robust and reminds of certain late imperial structures. It is interrupted to make way for a gateway to a garden and a stretch of a Roman road. Here also is the Museum's main entrance, with a marble lintel inscribed with the word which defines the institution, above which is a niche which houses a replica of the original sculpture. The double doors, on which there appears in bas-relief, the layout of known monuments in the city including that of the museum itself.

The south side, in keeping with its administrative role, adopts a more domestic appearance, in which the windows alternate between semicircular on the lower section and rectangular on the upper with, shutters on the latter.

On the east face the brickwork has some has outstanding features and as far as it is possible to make out, certain parts of the buildings internal structure are practically unimaginable from the outside.

Lastly, the north façade, extremely simple, with accentuated doorways breaking the monotony of the enormous lateral section.

"Genius of the Colony".

Image of Augustus.

The building is fundamentally divided into two sections: the exhibition area and the administration and services section. The two are connected by a gallery suspended above a Roman road.

Now inside the building a ramp leads to the Museum's main exhibition hall. Once past the doors of the great hall, we gaze in awe at this enormous space, with its huge arches, the roof of which is marked by skylights providing the natural light, which "inundates" every corner of the Museum. The main hall is, as already mentioned, of enormous proportions and in which there are as many as nine identical arches the dimensions of which are equal to the "Arco de Trajano", or Trojan Arch, one of the town's most remarkable monuments.

The ground floor contains two very different sections in addition to the central area: one to the left, which is both spacious and of an ideal configuration to exhibit large sculptures and mosaics and the other, to the right, in the form of a transversal aisle, in which, numerous pieces of all types are astutely exhibited either on pedestals or the walls themselves. The back of these lateral aisles an arch higher than that of the mean circumference demarcates a number of crypts, located behind a passage and scarcely visible from a distance, which prove to be a highly likely location for the outstanding pieces with sufficient appeal to draw the visitor to them.

An attempt has been made, of an eminently didactic nature, to reflect in each and every part of the Museum, throughout all three floors, the facets which defined every day life in this great western Roman city, *Augusta Emerita,* expounded as they are by evocative archaeological pieces.

The larger pieces are suitably arranged, either on granite pedestals or against the wall.

The display cabinets are of an exclusive design for the Museum and consist of a brass frame with unbreakable glass and a stucco base, in either Pompeian red or white. Those arranged on the ground floor also include a limestone pedestal and wooden base, the structure is such that they are

Statue of Cronos (left) and burial monument dedicated to Zósimo (above), in the Roman Museum.

Ground floor

On the ground floor, the idea has been to exhibit aspects of both official and private life in the colony.

Displayed in the first three areas or halls are features relating to the entertainment buildings, the Theatre, Amphitheatre, and the Circus, the relics of which constitute the most outstanding of Mérida's collection of monuments.

The areas to the left, by way of large cubicles, are occupied by sculptured monuments from excavations of the Theatre, three spaces united by beautiful arches from which a variety of perspectives can be obtained. Particularly remarkable is the statue of Pluto, actually a representation by Sérapis, the effigy of Ceres, set on a high pedestal presiding over the collection and the representations of emperors in military dress.

To the right, in the transversal aisle, hall I displays objects from the Amphitheatre and Circus: a plaque commemorating the inauguration of the Amphitheatre (8 BC), a restoration of the balustrade with paintings alluding to the games which took place in the arena, the inscription which recalls the Circus restoration between 337-340 AD., etc.

In hall II, everything has been included which is proven to be related to imperial homage. The celebrated gallery of imperial portraits: Augustus,

fully accessible to carry out any reformations or cleaning. There are also other types of cases and display stands in the form of tables, with wooden pedestals, where more or less flat pieces are exhibited such as window lights, objects in bone and ivory, gold and silver items, etc.

With regard to the information provided for visitors, it is simple and direct, with large panels which explain the general contents and small signs offering a descriptive summary of each the pieces.

Next, we move on to reveal the diverse aspects and different sections in the various halls.

Agrippina, Tiberius, Prince Julio-Claudio together with the altar and pedestals discovered in the theatre which constitute reasonable evidence of the propaganda and religious elements that were present in the monument.

Lastly, in hall III, the physical history of the Theatre, the exhibited architectural pieces and epigraphs which correspond and bear witness to its most notable restoration works.

Halls IV and V are dedicated to the religions. The varied populations which settled in *Emerita* explain the many religions which came into being here: the official State religions, that of the classic pantheon deity, those related to eastern gods and those which were genuinely indigenous.

Particularly outstanding are the sculptures and epigraphs found in the Mitra sanctuary, the zenith of which centred on the second half of the 2nd century AD, a brilliant period for the powerful personality *pater partum, Gaius Accius Hedychrus.* Aside from this, the magnificent mosaic by *Annibonius* of Baco and Ariadna, the effigy of the *genius Coloniae,* as well as other notable pieces including epigraphs of

Thoracata.

ℳ

gods, all of which constitute a fine collection. One significant piece in the display cabinet in hall V is the memorial dedicated to Proserpina, whose name was given to the reservoir where one of Méridas most outstanding dam systems originated.

Hall IV is taken up with funerary rites. Of the excavations carried out in burial sites around the town, numerous pieces have come to light which indicate various types of burials, both internments and cremations. Also of interest are a good number of commemorative plaques, altars, memorial stones and steles, all of which speak of various deceased personages and their circumstances, and also a *cuppa* and the tomb with its stepped plinth belonging to legionnaire Zósimo, quartermaster in the *Legio VII*.

As far as the Roman house in Mérida is concerned, an amazing pictorial collection can be seen which was recuperated from the excavations of a house next to calle Suárez Somonte. They are paintings of a type, the work of a good artisan not entirely devoid of artistic talent who well knew how to meet the wishes of his clients by reflecting the scenes most in vogue in the 4th century AD, the

ℳ

Mercury seated.

date which corresponds to the paintings: the circus and hunting. The collection is completed by the well-known *Rapto de Europa* mosaic together with those from the Roman *villa* "El Hinojal" in the "Las Tiendas" meadow, one of which is decorated with huge vases and the other, an interesting scene of a panther being hunted by a noble.

In the next area, and worthy of some attention, is a model recreating the layout of the colony of *Augusta Emerita*.

the bodies of which were the work of aristocratic Italic sculptor *Caius Aulus,* whose artistic skill is evident. Within the same collection are the clípeos and medallions with representations of Jupiter Ammon and Medusa, which decorated the upper floor of this portico, together with caryatids which flanked the aforementioned medallions. The setting for these unique pieces at the far end of the great hall is truly spectacular and could be said to be the Museum's "placard". The work involved in these

4th century paintings in the Roman Museum.

— ℳ —

Finally, halls VIII, IX an X have been assigned to the public life which developed around the forum. Excavations in the "Templo de Diana" and the adjoining portico have resulted in the discovery of important structures which give us a better idea of the character of this area designed as it was for the benefit of the citizens.

This monumental portico is a particularly outstanding feature of the forum. It is here the statues of those personages sporting togas appeared,

clípeos and caryatids can be perfectly appreciated by the public from the pieces on display in hall VIII. The exhibition is completed by capitals and different architectural elements from a colossal statue of the emperor in military dress.

Middle floor

This area is divided into nine halls, with subdued lighting and various display cabinets and exhibition shelves which are arranged along the walls, in two sections, which contain the small pieces which bear witness to the presence of industrial arts in *Emerita*.

*Mosaics in the Roman Museum. "Caza de Jabalí", (Wild Boar Hunting) "mosaico nilótico"
(mosaic depicting scenes from the Nile) and "Annibonius".*

Ceramics, glass, objects in bone, not forgetting a modest but significant collection of gold and silver items and the numismatics are all exhibited in great detail and with corresponding explanations.

Of particular interest are the Museum's glassware collections, in which it is possible to appreciate a variety of different types from over an extensive chronological period and which correspond either to those produced locally or well documented importations. We would particularly like to point out, though not dismissing other collections, the section containing items made of bone, which boasts a comprehensive selection of both objects and utensils.

Within the numismatics section are excellent examples of coins from the *Augusta Emerita* mint, of which the centre has a good selection of all kinds including numerous gold coins recently acquired on behalf of the Museum.

Equally interesting is the fairly accurate reconstruction of a *columbarium* complete with urns for the ashes of the deceased.

On this floor visitors can obtain information regarding the specification of the various objects exhibited and their uses, as well as details of how they were made and their commercial distribution.

Upper floor

The Museum's upper floor is designed to portray other collections in their context, which include memorials, sculptures and above all mosaics, all of which can be perfectly appreciated on this level, although there is an opportunity to see them on the ground and middle floors.

The brilliant light from above considerably enhances sculptured pieces, such as the busts from the school of *Emerita,* or the inscriptions on memorial and altar stones.

Other aspects of Roman life in *Augusta Emerita* are also displayed here on the Museum's top floor

Gold coin with Augustus.

and which are better understood with the help of the corresponding information duly provided.

Included in Hall I is an exhibition of those documents, more specifically epigraphs, which make reference to public office administration, both provincial and local. A small section explains the workings of the colony's water supply, including the name of one of its water supply systems *Agua Augusta*. The great "Las Tiendas" mosaic is a truly spectacular sight, both in terms of size and the quality of its central scene, which depicts wild boar hunting and busts of the four Seasons, perfectly setting the scene for this, the first of the halls on the upper floor.

The second section is set aside to present what is a little known reality: the territory of the *Augusta Emerita* colony. A graphic diagram in the hall illustrates the territorial limits in its entirety, the reality substantiated by various archaeological documents discovered during the excavation of a number of *villae.*

Merida's society is scrutinised, in as much as we are able to do so, in halls III and IV. The first contains a review of the origins of those who came to settle here, which is proven to be well varied. This society was involved in numerous activities. With respect to this, sources of information have been far from mediocre and from which we know the names of some of Mérida's celebrated personages, such as the poet Deciano, a reputable lawyer from Rome itself, but the most abundant source of information regarding the professions of these people is down to the epigraphs and tools which have appeared as a result of the excavations.

Perhaps one of the Museum's most outstanding collections is that of the busts, extraordinary works from the school of *Emerita*. The sculptors in *Emerita* worked practically without any interruption from when the city first came into being until the 5th century, proof of the thriving artistic element within the provincial population nucleus. We have already mentioned the powerful personality of *Gaius Aulus,*

Above, male portrait and stele of Lutatia Lupata. Below, to the right, mosaic of "Los Siete Sabios", (The Seven Wise Men).

officially commissioned by the forum and to whose name has to be added a good many artists, including *Demetrios* and others, though unnamed, also capable of truly the expressing art of these realistic portraits together with a subtle attempt to depict psychological aspects of the represented personage.

Halls V and VI contain exhibits relevant to this artistic trend, enhanced as they are by the abundance of natural light which floods these rooms, enabling the finest details of these effigies to be fully appreciated.

Naturally this exhibition couldn't exist without some account of intellectual life in *Augusta Emerita*, the demonstrations of which are evident throughout the entire Empire, but perhaps with more clarity during the 4th century AD. The representation of a Muse, a somewhat course piece of work, though not without skill, the mosaic of the "Siete Sabios" or Seven Wise Men, of unquestionable iconographic interest, the impression of the child *Lutatia Lupata* and various inscriptions, written in verse, are excellent proof of the mentality of the city's leading personalities.

Crypt in the Museo de Arte Romano.

Lastly, hall VIII, which is dedicated to Mérida's early Christian and Visigoth periods, and this centre's link with the town's future Visigoth Art and Culture Museum, a necessity to be able to exhibit this rich archaeological culture. The importance of *Augusta Emerita* as the Episcopal head, from the beginning of the 6th century, under the protection of its strong-willed bishops, made it possible, as a result of Mérida's popularity, for Hispano art in Visigoth times to flourish.

Beneath the exhibition area, conserved in a crypt, which in some ways remind us of the Roman arcaded crypts, are the ruins recuperated during the site's excavation. In addition to the previously mentioned road and a fair section of the "San Lázaro" water conduction system, preserved in a crypt which corresponds to a suburban area located close to the wall and which fundamentally consists of living quarters and a necropolis.

Of particular interest are the ruins of a house with its arcaded patio and well defined passages and rooms decorated with paintings, one of which illustrates two perfectly differentiated and superimposed phases. The house remains include the reconstructed courtyard with its columns.

Another two rooms are partly preserved, in the south-eastern corner of this remarkable archaeological site. This time, the focus is on a room in which the entrance is defined by two columns with parietal decoration. As regards the burial sites, various tombs were found from a period dating from the 1st to the 3rd century AD. The most significant find amongst the remains is a mausoleum with six burial sites, side by side.

The impressive architecture in this section, in which out of respect for archaeological standards the lighting is subdued, makes this considerable collection of remains rather evocative.

The floors of the other main section of the building are dedicated to everything involved with the Museum's administration and technical services: workshops, library, lecture theatre, etc.

Painting of the Monument to Santa Eulalia and one of the altar stones, now in the Roman Museum.

THE SANTA EULALIA MONUMENT

One of the monuments most unnoticed to the majority of the town's visitors is the one which was raised in memory of the patron saint of Mérida, made up of various elements including notable Roman pieces.

The first mention of the monument, as on so many other occasions, is that provided by the city's chronicler Bernabé Moreno de Vargas. In the year 1633, when his "History of the city of Mérida" first went to print, in which reference is made to a statue and other pieces of columns in the San Juan fields, which were used to erect a magnificent "needle". The origin of the said pieces is unknown. Moreno was given to understand that the altars came from the atrium of the so called temple of Diana, but there was nothing certain. We can, on the other hand, only try to imagine

The Santa Eulalia Monument.

how it could have ended up in a place so far from the town itself. The area of San Juan or Arrabal as it was also known, in the time of Mereno, was nothing more than a piece of open ground. What is certain is that some time must have passed before the idea took shape.

The appearance of a votive altar in red grained white marble, referring to the Concordia de Augosto, served to revitalise the outmoded idea of raising a monument to the patron saint of Mérida. The local authorities took the initiative to give the piece a clear site away from all those well-known. Supposedly, the appearance of the cited altar was news in tranquil 17th century Mérida with its six hundred habitants and even more so knowing that some

of its inhabitants had stolen the altar and moved it to their home. It was actually the son of Moreno de Vargas himself who insisted on it being recuperated. It was then it was believed, conveniently so, that this piece, together with others of great importance and ancient craftsmanship, according to the Historic Municipal Archives, from the time, "originally formed part of a pyramid", and was to be raised on steps, on the top of which was to be "the representation of the image Santa Eulalia".

The work began, beneath the auspices of the town, with the construction of a terrace five steps high, on top of which was the base with the letters of the Concordia de Augosto, three cylindrical altars, two of which were beautifully decorated with bucráneos (skulls of sacrificed bulls), garlands and instruments of Roman liturgy, a capital, a block with three coat of arms, those of the Crown, Mérida and the governor- and a plaque inscribed with: "The town of Mérida, governed by Field Marshal don Lope de Tordoya y Figueroa, nobleman of the Orden de Santiago erected this monument to the town's patron saint Santa Eulalia in the year MDCLII". The monument is crowned by the white marble image of the martyr Santa Eulalia.

The people of Mérida were only able to enjoy this new masterpiece for a short time before it began to show signs of its poor construction work, having to be restored in 1661.

At the end of the 19th century, whilst Pedro María Plano was in office, it was agreed to restore the affected parts with marble mortar at the same time as it would be moved from its original position to another 40 metres higher, replacing the steps by a stone pedestal, the corners decorated with Tuscan columns and the facades adorned with garlands in keeping with the workmanship of those pieces it was to support.

The monument has at the present time been taken down due to the urban modernisation project underway in the vicinity and the pieces are currently exhibited in the Museo Nacional de Arte Romano. Copies have been made of the monuments various pieces which will be raised again in the Rambla de la Mártir Santa Eulalia.

TEMPLO DE MARTE

Leaving the Santa Eulalia obelisk behind us in front of the Santa Eulalia church, some 200 metres on, by the side of the old road to Madrid, (see in the chapter Modern Mérida), are the remains of the Templo de Marte.

In reality, nothing is known of the original structure, nor where it was first sited, since what has been conserved are some of its remains which were used in a portico constructed in Mérida in the 17th century, in front of a chapel which is believed to be in remembrance of the martyred saint's last resting place, in the time of Emperor Diocleciano. Information about the period from whence came these ruins is, unfortunately, somewhat scarce; an inscription from the left corner of the architrave states: "These carved marble stones were found amongst this town's ruins". The original pieces of exceptional construction included: two sections of marble columns, of different diameters and the two Corinthian capitals, also in marble, placed on top, plus six architraves, one of which, in former times served as a step, and is now in the Museum, and finally a cornice, the remaining pieces being replications added during construction in the 17th century.

Detail on the Temple.

Remains of the Templo de Marte in front of Santa Eulalia.

Much admired for their artistic value are the pieces of architrave, the fronts of which are decorated with a frieze adorned with the heads of medusas in the form of medallions, combined with floral elements and palms. The surface below is decorated with a selection of the apparel and armaments appertaining to Roman armies: decorated shields, all types of weapons, cartwheels, warlike symbols, military ensigns, etc., in the centre of which are medallions bearing the trophies of war.

The ornamentation is broken in the centre of the frieze by an epigraph which tells of the temple's dedication to Marte by Vetila, the wife of Páculo (MARTI SACRUM VETTILLA PACULI), possibly in the time of Antoninos, since around that time, Páculo, from the noble senatorial Roscios family, was probably the governor of Lusitania, and as such, resident in the city. Lower down still, another modern inscription, also in Latin, reminds us that the monument is not only dedicated to Marte but also to Jesus Christ and the martyr Eulalia. To finish, another inscription, this time in Spanish, tells us that in 1612, the city of Mérida at the time when Luis Manrique de Lara was governor, rebuilt this chapel with the aid of alms, the name of which was "Hornito de Santa Eulalia", by which it is still known today.

Remains of the Roman Baths.

THE ROMAN BATHS BUILDING ON CALLE REYES HUERTAS

Located in its original setting in a district outside the city centre, surrounded by an extensive necropolis and almost next to the Casa del Anfiteatro, excavations began in 1927 instigated by José Ramón Mélida, only to be left forgotten until the new project began in 1981, the result of which is as it is found today.

The building, the remains of which are still half buried by the surrounding hamlet, accommodated in its day some type of thermal baths or rather industrial building, although from times of old, on account of its proximity to the Christian necropolis adjacent to the Santa Eulalia basilica, it was thought it might bear some relation to the first Christian cults, albeit in its orthodox or heretical branch, even though there has been no mention of mitraicos cults.

What is visible today consists of, on the lower level, three huge concrete foundations, a quadrangle with eight steps down, which is connected to, via a small door, another octagonal and linked to a third by means of a subterranean passage 13 metres long. This third and most interesting example is round with a 7.20 metre diameter, the vault of which there remains only a circular ledge, in the centre of which eight circular granite pillars have been preserved, arranged in a circle around a dry stone parapet, now almost completely disappeared. Another

similar passage, 2 metres long, leading in a north easterly direction ends is finished by a wall with a niche; a third, opposite the first, leads to a room 4 metres by 5, walled in to the east in the form of an apse but open on the west side by an evenly sloping passage which comes out at a well, 2.5 metres in diameter and 8 metres deep. The entire room is covered by a semicircular vault with exterior ventilation provided by three chimneys. As regards the decoration, this amounts to some barely visible stucco work. On the upper level, around the rotunda and even breaking into part of the original structure, the remains of hot baths are still visible, with their corresponding *hypocausta,* with which we imagine that, if not in its perhaps industrial beginnings, the building was with the passing of time, adapted for the use of thermal baths possibly towards the end of the 3rd or beginning of the 4th century.

THE COLONY'S FORUM

Accurately identifying the forum in the colony of *Augusta Emerita* has never been easy, even though the local erudite placed it in the exact location it effectively occupies. It was during the course of excavations carried out on the "Templo de Diana" when it became possible to establish its location. Equally the building's orientation with its south facing main façade as the former discoveries referred to by local historians, makes it appear that the site of the forum was between the present day

Painting by De Laborde, showing the Templo de Diana.

calle Sant José and Los Maestros, on the one side and the "Templo de Diane" and calle Viñeros on the other. Later findings have provided a more accurate definition of this extraordinary place which extends as far as the present day calle de Cimbrón and Brudo.

The structural layout is common to Roman cities in the west at the time of the first imperial rule.

"Casa de los Milagros", or house of miracles, the reason for which we find the temple in such an excellent state. Being periptero and hexastyle, orientated roughly north to south. The temple's rectangular layout is of 40.75 metres on the sides and 21.90 metres on the front and back. It is constructed entirely of granite stone, from the hillsides of "Proserpina".

The site includes a temple, that of "Diana" and a range of buildings which complete the temple to the south, some of which were discovered recently in calle Dávalos Altamirano.

The most significant of the ensemble is the "Templo de Diana" together with an arcade, ideologically attached to the religious building.

The temple site became occupied in the 16th century by a rather singular mansion, the so-called

Templo de Diana.

M

The colonnade rests on a base 3.23 metres high, from the top to the base of the plinth.

The longest sides boast a total of eleven stuccoed columns set on bases without plinths, likewise the drums which formed the shafts. The

Two views of the Forum's Portico and a view of the Renaissance palace located next to the Temple of Diana.

Corinthian capitals are comprised of a triple acanthus crown as well as being decorated with fine stucco work.

The pieces of architrave which support the roof are particularly well preserved. The main façade has recently been restored including the pediment, the tympanum of which contained a support arch, not visible at the time.

The main south facing entrance opens on to a forum with a small raised section or stage, by way of a *rostra,* from where the staircase begins which accessed the building.

Around the temple is a sacred area or *temenos,* part of which it has been possible to reinstate. This gardened area is finished with a portico.

As regards the construction date, architectural features together with data collected during excavation points to it being set around the beginning of the Tiberius period.

The portico, discovered at the end of the last century and researched rather more recently, is further proof of the extent to which historic monuments were created in *Augusto Emerita.*

There was a large landscaped area surrounded by a monumental portico, the upper level of which is interestingly embellished with clípeos or medallions with alternating heads of Jupiter Ammón and Medusa, separated, in the style of metopes, by caryatids, very much in keeping with other Italic examples, amongst which are those of the Foro de Augosto, the Augustus forum. The central area is made up walkways or footpaths paved with marmoreal stone. Finally, an entire iconographical world presents itself in rectangular sections, distributed over the grounds interior wall, part of which was the work of local sculptor *Gaius Aulus,* which includes effigies of notable personages from Roman history, members of the imperial house and sculptural groups which bring to mind the relation of the Augustus family with divine personages, in this case the goddess Venus, mother of the Trojan hero Aeneas, the central character in an extraordinary scene on the portico, depicting his flight from Troy with his father Anquises on his shoulders, hand in hand with his son, Ascanio and other well known personages which now appear exhibited in the Museo Nacional de Arte Romano.

Bronze sculpture of the Genius of the Senate.

EL ARCO DE TRAJANO

Immersed as it is within the midst of modern constructions, masked by neighbouring houses, the Arco de Trajano, or Trojan Arch rises majestically out of all this, to be the historical monument most admired by both travellers and historians throughout the ages.

Its denomination is purely arbitrary and merely the response to a popular whim.

To tell the truth, we have no knowledge of which emperor was in power at the time it was raised, although it can be said, at the risk of being wrong, that according to the construction techniques, it is a typical construction from the time of Augustus.

Constructed entirely of granite, the strength of this structure is enviable. Set on top of the sturdy stone supports are as many as 23 arch stones. The height is 13.79 metres and the width 5.70 metres with the arch span covering 8.67 metres.

Etching of the Arco de Trajano and on the opposite page, a general present day view of the same.

— 𝔐 —

The arch must have had a very different appearance in ancient times from what we see today. Either side of the central opening would have been another two, of noticeably smaller dimensions. The holes on certain ashlars indicate that they would have been dressed in marble, although it has to be said that many of these orifices were simply to attach the hooks which served to raise the heavy blocks.

Since the 18th century, when Villena Mosiño carried out an excavation of the site and drew up a plan and elevation of the arch, it was believed to be one of the main arteries of the city's road network, the one which ran from north to south *(kardo),* passing beneath the arch. We don't know whether he wanted to offer an independent interpretation of what he saw, or whether he was simply mistaken, since no such road passed beneath the arch, but a beautiful marble floor and the start of a base for the steps of a monumental staircase leading to the doors of the temple recently discovered in calle Holguín, are a determining factor as regards investigating the most difficult aspect of the monument, that of its function.

If it was initially thought that its structure could be compared with that of ancient trophies, although very soon support was given to the theory that it could be treated as none other than one of the gateways to the colony, the very same which appeared on coins minted in the city and the emblem of the same. Mérida worked on the theory of an *urbs quadrata* or a primitive foundational enclosure which had followed the examples introduced by the Roman heirarchy. The urban layout came to be determined by two main routes, *kardo* and *decumanus máximus,* at the extremes of which were raised monumental gateways of which the Trojan arch would have been one.

There is a second theory which defends the triumphal configuration, architected as it was by Moreno de Vargas and his strongest supporter, Richmond. This theory brought about a new and in our opinion definitive interpretation, according to which, the arch served as the foyer to a public enclosure of great importance, the main forum, the public square where the buildings were located which attended to the needs of the public administrators to the Province and of which *Augusta Emerita* was the capital.

The arch's noble stature and grandeur were enough in themselves to identify an area, the evidence of which was duly supported. The arch also played an important role in the integration of different areas within the city itself.

TEMPLO DE CULTO IMPERIAL

The appearance of what was in its day one of the most magnificent temples in the *colonia Augusta Emerita,* in calle Holguín, in an area where for centuries they have been continuously documenting an important collection of findings, has finally confirmed the hypothesis that in and around the ancient Plaza de Santiago, now known

— 𝔐 —

Remains of the Temple on calle Holguín.

as the Plaza de la Constitution, was the site of one of the city's public areas, very likely the provincial Forum. A good part of the temple's podium remains encased within the neighbouring buildings. Constructed in concrete *(opus caementicium)* adorned with granite ashlars and according to the most recent archaeological findings, we are able to say that the podium would have had been a maximum of 38 metres long, of which 20 corresponded to the *cella*. The height of the podium amounted to around 3.50 metres. Some architectural pieces from the temple have been recuperated during archaeological excavations including marmoreal tambours and crown mouldings from the columns.

The temple was accessed by means of a staircase or alternatively a ramp which started from the so called Arco de Trajano and led to the entrance of the same. This meant in effect that a stretch of the *kardo maximus* had to be closed and what were then domestic properties had to be demolished, in order to construct the temple and its plaza.

An analysis of the design from some of the building's architectural pieces deduces it to be from the time of Tiberius, a claim confirmed by geological studies of the rock strata. This dating is also reaffirmed by the appearance of the temple in monumental epigraphs and the representation of the temple on coins from the local mint in Mérida, where the coins were dedicated to the Eternity of Augustus. Everything, without exception, points to the fact that the temple was consecrated to the imperial cult, though still to be determined is whether it was at the initiative of the colony or the province.

The temple's design is along metropolitan lines, more specifically those of the temple of Concordia and perhaps, as has been conjectured, L. Fulcinio Trión may have had a hand in the temple's construction, being the governor of the province of Lusitania in the time of Tiberius.

ROMAN HOUSES

The knowledge of residential houses or "casas" in Roman Mérida is, in reality, extremely fragmented. It is true that within the urban district remains of mansions have been found which contain mosaics, some of which are exhibited in the Museum, but it is no less certain that what is known about the structure of these residences is minimal. Nevertheless, examples preserved, most of all from suburban mansions, provide us with an acceptable overview of the evolution of Mérida's residential architecture from the 1st century AD until well into the fourth century.

Generally, houses were built around a central patio surrounded by a covered passage onto which the main rooms would open. Some were of particularly spectacular dimensions, as is the case of the existing one next to the Amphitheatre. All being fine manifestations of architecture and of the ornamentation which decorated their walls and floors: essentially frescoes and mosaics.

In addition to those discovered in calle Suárez Somonte and in the "Huerta de Otero" garden, now no longer visible, there are those of the Alcazaba, that of the Teatro and above all the "Casa del Anfiteatro" and the "Casa del Mitreo" which are the most outstanding.

The house on the inside of the Alcazaba or citadel is classed as a *domus,* in which the main rooms are arranged around the central courtyard, amongst which is the *oecus* or sitting room, with an excellent floor which appeared to be tiled in marble of a geometric design *(opus sectile)* and some *cubicula* or small rooms complete with ornamental mosaics, also a feature in the passages or corridors. Two periods in the life of the house can be determined, one relating to the 2nd century AD, to which some of the mosaics and the marble floor are attributed and the other, the 4th century AD.

Of particular interest are the remains of the house dubbed by those who discovered it as "Casa-Basílica", due to the presence of apses, located at the head of its main rooms. The character of the house, in truth, is a long way from being considered a Christian oratorio, the apse in this case being typical of domestic Roman architecture. From this period came the excellent wall frescoes with representations of personages dressed in ankle length robes. By contrast, the mosaics discovered beneath those which are to be seen on the covered terrace are from a former period, the 2nd century AD, the date associated with the original construction of the house. The house occupied part of the theatre's patio garden and arcaded terrace.

The "Casa del Anfiteatro"

Named as such due to its location next to this monument, it is, in reality, made up of two houses: one known as the "Casa de la Torre de Agua", the name of which comes from its position next to the water deposit for the "San Lázaro" water supply system, and the strictly speaking "Casa del Anfitheatre".

What remains preserved of the first is reduced to two rooms which open on to a patio and covered terrace which is almost completely destroyed, as is the rest of what was the mansion.

The first of the rooms, badly preserved though it is, was of a rectangular design with a black and white mosaic floor from the end of the 1st century or beginning of the 2nd century AD. From this room it is possible to access the next, set on a slightly higher level and in which the remains of a mosaic are conserved, similar to that of the neighbouring chamber.

The walls of these rooms have retained some painted stucco work, designed to simulate marble

Casa del Anfiteatro. Mosaic of the Grape Harvest.

stones of a rectangular form which alternated with rhomboidal shapes.

Of the patio there remains very little to be seen, two brick columns, covered with stucco work and part of the small channel which originally ran the length of its perimeter.

South of this patio, other parts of the house included another patio and more rooms.

It has been possible to date this house according to excavation findings. Construction dates back to the 1st century AD, the house not existing beyond the 3rd century AD, when it was substituted by the "Casa del Anfiteatro".

Next to the house a particularly good stretch of the wall from Roman colonial times can be seen, also the aforementioned water deposit for the aqueduct and a spring with the head of a lion decorating the water pipe.

Casa del Anfiteatro.

--------------------------------- ℳ ---------------------------------

The "Casa del Anfitheatro" is of surprisingly large proportions, which some have tried to explain, without any supporting evidence, as it having been intended as some sort of education or training centre for young people or alternatively for a semi-official purpose.

The house's construction, in accordance with the tile designs and other details, dates back to the end of the 3rd century AD, its final days agreed to be some time during the 5th century, this being the time the necropolis was established on the same site. Its location was classed as suburban, that is to say outside the walled part of the city, next to the street which passed by the Amphitheatre.

Nowadays the house is entered by a wide door, which has absolutely nothing to do with the original version. Next to this is a large quadrangular room paved in bricks with lime mortar with the remains of plaster on its walls. From what was probably a vestibule, it would have been possible to access the house's large covered passage and patio, around which the most important rooms would have been arranged.

The patio with its surrounding portico or covered passage was supported by granite columns, in the centre of which, was a garden *(viridarium)*. Of the passage, three of the four wings display mosaic tiled floors with ornamental

and geometric designs whilst the fourth presents a floor made of brick and lime mortar. The principal rooms opened onto these passages.

To the right are two almost identical rooms with floors of hydraulic mortar and the remains of painted stucco work on the walls. The west wing passage accessed part of the mansion which was on a higher level and where a number of rooms were located. The best preserved both have brick and lime mortar floor surfaces and open on to a small passage. It was discovered that the interior walls were decorated with pictorial paintings, sadly in a poor state of conservation, with imitation marble plinths.

Still in the west wing passage, we can admire the mosaic which decorated its floor with a frame created by a simple cable twine rope and a central geometrical interlinked pattern. Other rooms could be accessed from the passage which also had brick and lime mortar floors.

Continuing our tour, we come to the south wing passage, with a mosaic identical to that seen on the inside. This wing was made up of a variety of rooms. The larger rooms had a grand appearance, one in particular, probably a *triclinium* or dining room, includes an interesting pictorial and iconographic mosaic, possibly created at the hands of a painter named *Quintosus,* whose signature it bore up until some years ago, now no longer visible due to the lamentable state of the building's conservation.

The mosaic's background is made up of red, black and white squares and set squares; the central scene, divided into two parts, displays the figures of Venus and Cupid in one of the squares and in the other a winepress whereby three workers can be seen treading grapes, the residue of which is shown being collected in three fat containers. Around the scene are others depicting aspects of the fruit collecting process at the hands of little cupids who climbed the grapevines with ladders, whilst others transported the bunches to the winepress.

The work involved in the mosaic is sure to be of interest, restoration work carried out throughout the ages is clearly visible with mosaic tiles of a lighter shade than those originally used.

A passage leads to other parts of the house and rooms with mortar bases, though not yet excavated in their entirety. The passage itself contains a mosaic displaying a decorative motif made up of two-tone squares, with two red and black triangular sections, each one alternating with white squares which create the figure of an hourglass.

The next section of the same passage displays another mosaic floor to muse over with a field of red black and white rhombus shapes.

The passage comes into another, though wider, equally with a mosaic tiled floor. The decorative motif in this case is a diagram of a succession of white circles surrounded by double H's or united jacks around a curved square. Both passage and mosaic are repeated on the opposite side of the house.

This passage takes us to the spacious anteroom or vestibule to a large room in which there is a wealth of introspective decoration, with a meandering patterned border and five well defined sections: those at the ends, with emblems and those in the centre, with squared medallions, with a labyrinth of rope in the centre flanked by two triangular and two rhomboidal roses. In the corners of the squares containing the roses are fissures and in those containing the labyrinth motif, towering structures.

The vestibule is completed by another passage with a mosaic in the form of squares arranged in shades of red, black, white-red and black-white.

The aforementioned room, next to the vestibule, is in fact the largest in the house. Its role as a reception room seems quite clear although it could also have been, judging by the mosaic tiling, that of the *triclinium* or dining room.

The mosaic comprises a border which emulates large red and black tiled squares with small black squares on a white background. The central scene portrays a design made up of squares of crossed cable, creating eight pointed stars which demarcate octagonal medallions in between which are small diamond and octagonal shapes. The space created by the crossed squares is filled with circles framed by waves, in the centre of which diverse marine species are depicted, some of which can be identified, sea bream, hake, conger eel, lobster, sole, moray eel and grouper.

The final section of the house, judging by what we are able to see today, consists of more rooms with mosaic tiled floors alongside a passage which it appears also has a mosaic floor covered with flowers which have four petals and circles each bearing the Malta cross.

Casa del Mitreo. Peristyle.

The whole ensemble is completed by chambers of an apparently thermal nature, which were established alongside the wall of the "San Lázaro" water pipe. The remains of the infrastructure *(hypocaustum)* of a room intended to provide hot baths *(calidarium)*, includes a pool and the stove *(praefurnium)* which heated the water, together with annexes.

Of the rooms next to the hot baths, one worthy of mention is the kitchen with its fireplace and various pieces of equipment.

The "Casa del Mitreo"

This house was given its name on account of its proximity to the ruins of a sanctuary dedicated to Mitre and the eastern gods and was discovered at the beginning of the seventies, during the construction of the adjacent plaza de Toros. Some thought it may have been the priest's mansion from the aforementioned sanctuary, or even that it was part of the sanctuary itself, of which there still remain many unknown factors as regards its exact location. In any event, its location was equally suburban.

The house appears to have been constructed at the end of the 1st or beginning of the 2nd century AD, to be later abandoned probably some time during the 4th century AD.

Various parts of the structure of this magnificent building can be determined, although the present day entrance bears no relation to the original.

The first nucleus appears to have developed around a central garden *(viridarium)* and covered patio and a pond endowed with the habitual exedras. Surrounded as it was by passages which, in their day, would been tiled with mosaics, of which now there remains only the vestiges in the west wing, and distributed from these passages, the rooms about to be described.

The three most significant include two smaller rooms of similar dimensions which flanked the main room, which probably served as a *triclinium*. The walls of the smaller rooms contain plinths one of which is interestingly decorated with plants and birds, though there remains little of the original work. The one to the right of the main room has a mosaic tiled floor

"Mosaico Cósmico" detail.

divided into three parts in which the central scene is surrounded by a combination of triangles, rhombi and squares in two sizes. The work dates back to the 2nd century AD as does that of the adjacent rooms. The room to the left presents various borders decorated with fretwork and meandering patterns and a central scene depicting a square filled with a meandering geometrical pattern. A carpet can still be seen at the entrance with its pattern containing stars with four points. The main room displays another mosaic which comprises a decorative border of squares and two carpets also of a geometrical design with a decorative border bearing the same motif. Next to these are other rooms in ruins.

In the west passage, along with the remains of a mosaic, patterned with squares and rectangles is a large cistern above which is another room, the excavations of which have produced some valuable pictorial pieces, now in the Museum's reserves room.

Already visible are some rooms off the south passage, one of which contains an interesting mosaic floor tiling depicting the figure of Eros with a dove in his hands.

Continuing our tour, we come to an area from where a staircase, the walls of which are decorated with an imitation veined marble effect, leads to two rooms, the purpose of which is yet to be defined, though it is thought they may have been used for rest periods during the summer season *(cubicula diurna)*.

At the end of the house, next to a road which, apparently, must be a prolongation of the colony's *kardo maximus,* there are some thermal installations, the remains of which include the oven, some brickwork foundations *(hypocaustum),* some hot water baths and their respective room *(calidarium),* with mosaic tiled flooring, patterned with squares and set squares.

Another wing of the house is arranged around a peristilo with a pond, surrounded by columns decorated with painted stuccos.

From the peristilo we are able to access the area where the house's original north entrance was located. Visible here is a staircase of granite ashlars which solved the problem of the difference in levels between the entrance and a tetra-style atrium around which various rooms were distributed. The small atrium *(atriolum),* with granite columns contained a small pond or *impluvium* decorated with marble mouldings.

Still to be suitably excavated are a series of rooms, the doors to which, with their granite door posts, are visible on the atrium's east side. On the opposite side, well centred in relation to the atrium, is a room where the "Mosaico Cósmico" was discovered, probably one of the most important in the Roman's world. Inside the room's construction features are perfectly visible: dry stone plinth of adobe construction reinforced with ashlars on the corners. The walls were decorated with paintings which in some areas have been preserved.

The mosaic depicts a complete illustration of the Cosmos, according to the legend from Hellenist times. The composition is presided over by the figure of Old Father Time and his sons, Heaven and Caos, next to the Titans, sons of the Heaven, the Earth: the Celestial Pole and the Thunder, surrounded by the figures of the Sun, the Moon, the Winds and the Clouds. In the centre of the Mosaic is *Aion,* the representation of Eternity, next to Nature, the Seasons, the Mountain and the Snow.

Exceptionally outstanding, also in the centre of the composition, is the beautiful figure of *Oriens,* Aurora, mounted on her four-in-hand, prepared to make her daily journey across the firmament.

"Mosaico Cósmico" general view.

On the bottom section, depicted amidst radiant shades of blue and green are the aquatic personifications: the rivers Nile and Euphrates, a Port, the Lighthouse, the Sea and Navigation.

Everything in the composition is perfect: the drawing quality, the subtle shades of the human figures, the colours of the different areas of the mosaic, etc. The different elements of nature also appear identified by their Latin names. The materials used to create this work of art were of the highest quality, even to the extent of using transparent glass tiles laminated with gold to emphasise various ornamental accessories on the figures, such as torques and bracelets or the crown worn by the beautiful figure of *Oriens.*

All is purely allegory; a simple means of explaining the phenomenon of nature.

On the outside of the room, the remains of pictorial decoration can be seen on the walls.

Taking a granite staircase leads us to the next section, where, on the right hand side, we can appreciate another remarkable part of the house: known as the "habitación de las pinturas", or the paintings room, named as such for its well preserved and excellent pictorial decoration. The plinth is decorated with foliage and birds, whilst the centre of the wall is filled with various pictures separated by motifs with candelabras.

Site of the "Columbarios" and one of the paintings.

— ℳ —

"LOS COLUMBARIOS" BURIAL SITE

Named as such by virtue of the two unusual outdoor burial monuments *(busta)*, excavated by D. J. R. Mélida and D. M. Macías in 1926, in the Nécropolis Oriental de Mérida as it was called, the idea being to bring us closer to the reality of the world of Roman burials by means of an extraordinary study centre containing the preserved remains.

The Centro de Interpretación or study centre revolves around two family burial monuments, that of the Julios family and that of the Voconia family. Being cremation burial sites, the lintels still bear the names of those whose ashes are contained within; on the one hand Cayo Voconio, of the Papyri tribe who dedicated the monument to his family (his father, mother and sister), and on the other the couple who married as free persons Cayo Julio Felix, Felix and Maoriola and their son Cayo Julio Modesto, who passed away at the early age of 27 years.

The Julios family mausoleum conforms to the usual trapezoidal design, to which a triangular structure has been added to its west side, with facings in granite ashlars, though of a lower height, which it seems was later added to and which may possibly have served as an *ustrinum*. The original part was constructed of strong *opus incertum* facings with a small door framed by granite blocks, crowned with merlones. Inside, on the wall to the left, is an *arcosolium* with quadrangular niches in which are the remains of urns containing the ashes of the deceased, beneath which is a large granite pew inside which another collection of funeral urns would have been safeguarded. Opposite the entrance is another niche, also quadrangular, with the remains of some pictorial decoration, which perhaps in its day, served to represent some of its most recent inhabitants.

The Voconios tomb was erected directly in front, the family being native of Arricia, on the Italic peninsula. The tomb is of a simple quadrangular structure with similar construction features to that of the Julios family. In his inscription over the door lintel, by way of an explicit announcement and not without some pride, Cayo Vocionio displays in outstanding semi-bas-relief of military decorations acquired during an extensive military career: two torques, two armbands *(armillae)*, in the form of a serpent, and between those, a framework of leather strips which serve to support the nine medals *(phalerae)*, typical military rewards for a soldier risen from the lowest ranks to become a centurion. On the inside, neatly stuccoed in white, three rectangular niches house the ashes and pictorial representations of the deceased. Opposite the entrance, the largest, with two funeral urns,

The bridge over the Guadiana and its cutwaters.

𝔐

probably those of the parents, Cayo and Cecilia, conventionally displayed upright on a basement pedestal facing the onlooker, the man, complete with toga and the woman sporting a cloak and tunic, To one side, a young woman, certainly Voconia María, and on the other a young bearded man, who, with almost the same certainty, was the same Cayo Voconio Próculo who had the monument erected in the time of Flavius, in the well known style of the Roman world and still visible today in well know archaeological sites such as the one in Ostia.

These mausoleums, together with many other various types of burials, make up an extensive burial ground located around one of the roads which left the city in the direction of ancient *Corduba,* now known as the "Área funeraria de los Columbarios", inaugurated as such in 2003 by the Consorcio de la Ciudad Monumental de Mérida, with the objective of conveying, by re-creating diverse interpretative techniques, from exhibiting and reproducing archaeological pieces, to reconstructing archaeological elements including

the latest advances resulting from archaeological investigations of Mérida's site regarding knowledge of the funeral world, equally with respect to the Roman concept of death as the way it was dealt with, the choice of burial site, the funeral rites and its evolution through time, or the means of perpetuating the memory of the deceased for generations to come.

THE BRIDGE OVER THE GUADIANA RIVER

The bridge or Puente over the river Guadiana, probably the most ancient of all the monuments visible in the city today, was constructed, in accordance with suitable topography, in a place where there existed a ford, a determining factor in establishing the colony in its early days and perhaps in successive periods until well into the 1st century AD. The existing bridge is 792 metres long.

Night view of the bridge over the Guadiana river.

The bridge was constructed of three sections of arches joined together, the first and second by a section protected by an enormous cutwater.

The first section of the stonework included the stretch between the Guadiana river dam and the present day main ramp and constitutes this work's best preserved section, being situated on the minor branch of the river and thus less exposed to the river's violent currents. A total of 10 arches were built to cross this stretch, supported by 9 foundation piles with rounded cutwaters, eight of which are particularly well preserved. The supporting piles are themselves perforated by overflows or small arches to relieve the flow of the current when the river rises.

The second section runs from the present day buttress piles, constructed in the 19th century, almost to the second descent ramp. Lastly, the third section covered the remaining stretch of the construction. The arches, including those constructed in the 17th century, amount to 60 in total.

The arch supports and arches up to the second descent ramp are identical to those described in the first section, whilst from the said ramp the support piles contain neither overflows nor dykes, easily explained by the fact that water only came to this zone during the big floods.

The bridge's construction consists of a strong concrete core with granite stone facings, probably from the quarries of Proserpina. The ashlars on the tympanums form a very regular line and join up with the arch stones and also with those of the small overflow arches. The bevelled edged ashlars noticeably break the monotony of the tympanums and create a frankly notable chiaroscuro effect. Returning to the piles, these are rectangular and of a considerable width, equally on account of the arch spans they were to support as for the precarious foundations in some places. The buttresses as previously mentioned are rounded, but in the modern parts of the construction they adopt a pyramidal structure, corresponding to alterations made in the 17th century and conical in the 19th century section.

The arches extend from a projecting impost, on a small ledge, or row of capping stones on the piles. The resulting arch stones are even with a well defined keystone. The outflow is quite distinct with its outfall channel well in evidence, although it doesn't extend beyond the surface of the tympanums.

There remains practically nothing of the bridge's original cornice, which capped the rows of ashlars and marked the start of the parapet.

One truly exceptional aspect of the bridge's architecture constituted a dyke which protected a breakwater connecting the two sections of arches. The ruins can still be seen today scattered amongst the river's gravel island, upstream, the result of its destruction over the centuries. The description from Moreno de Vargas, a local 17th century historian, helps to give us some idea of its strength: "It had a long wall and barrier up river, constructed with a bow rather like that of the upper section of a galley, to take the full force of the river's rapid current during normal and high water rises, so that by the time it reached the bridges it was rather more docile… As far as the bridge's safety was concerned there was equal space for pavement and road."

A construction on the scale of what was a predominantly functional bridge, the Puente de Mérida, was subjected to a great deal of damage provoked by floods and wars which were immediately rectified in as much as it was possible during the relevant eras. Thanks to documents preserved in the Municipal Historic Archives, there is supporting evidence of some of the restoration works carried out.

Amongst the most significant, we can highlight those carried out during the Visigoth period in the year 483, during the reign of Euric, of which we are reminded by an inscription now lost, also those in Arabian times and those in the 16th, 17th and 19th centuries. The most extensive correspond to those of the 17th century, when the bridges, following the destruction of the buttresses, were reunited by nine new arches and also those of the 19th century, the time which corresponds to a particularly good section of the construction.

The bridge begins with a modern parapet, with ashlar facings, lengthways on and a new cornice. Two overflows, reconstructed in the last century, denote a fair demonstration of the force of the waters during floods. Next are the four arches which span the flow of water.

Each arch presents the same features, fairly well preserved. They are each of a perfect semicircle, the spans of which vary between 5.20 m for the first and 3.80 m for the fourth. The arches extend from a base, as is the case of those on the Puente del Guadiana, though this time less evident. They are formed by a

THE ALBARREGAS BRIDGE

Base and elevation of the bridge over the Albarregas river.

The bridge over the Albarregas river (known as *Barraeca* in Roman times), the source of which is in the vicinity of the "Cornalvo" reservoir, though of less importance than that of the Guadiana, has had less influence in respect to the city's historic monuments, information regarding its history being somewhat scarce. Likewise any restoration work carried out on the structure has been poorly documented.

The road known as the "Via de la Plata" began from here and its orientation in some way determined the *kardo maximus* highway in *Emerita*.

The bridge nowadays extends some 145 metres, including the modern restoration works, whilst the width of the road is around 8 metres.

variable number of arch stones, the keystone of which is well defined and the mouthpiece barely perceptible. Some of the arch stones display reinforcing.

The supporting piles, with well structured facings, mostly eleven rows wide, have neither dykes nor overflows, being deemed unnecessary. The tympanums or wall area between on arch and another, are for the most part well conserved, the bevelled edged ashlars, perfectly aligned with the arch stones.

The Bridge, which can be dated to the period of change or the early decades of the 1st century AD, is completed by another parapet, modern for the best part, with dry-stone facings.

6 metres including the parapets. Numerous restoration works have visibly distorted something of its original character, although on the upstream section, its construction features are well visible, similar to the two previously described examples from Mérida.

ℳ

The "Alcantarilla Romana" (top left) and the dam (below).

THE "ALCANTARILLA ROMANA"

A third bridge was built by the Romans in Mérida, on the road which led to *Olisipo* (Lisbon), some 500 metres from the district know as "Las Abadías" and close to the bridge over the Albarregas, between kilometres 454 and 455 of the railway track to Badajoz.

With a single archway, the bridge is 7 metres long by 4.35 metres wide, which extends to

The construction core is concrete and the arch, bevelled edged granite arch stones, which rise from lightweight foundations made of ashlars. The arch span covers 4.20 metres. The interior vaulted section consists of brickwork.

The parapet is modern, as are also some parts of the construction. It is easy to appreciate the qualities of the Roman road, subsequently rebuilt, on the bridge itself and the surrounding area.

THE GUADIANA DAM

Those planning the layout of the *colonia Augusta Emerita* knew perfectly well the course of the river Guadiana (Ana) and, having observed the numerous floods following periods of heavy rainfall, they decided to create some form of protection from the water's assault by constructing a dam along the river bank, the remains of which are a powerful reminder of the erudite of bygone times.

The dam itself consists of a substantial wall in *opus mixtum,* with neat dry-stone walling and granite ashlars in five longitudinal courses. The wall is demarcated every so often by the presence of buttresses on various stretches. Constructed in ashlars and dry-stone, the courses of which alternate perfectly between a lengthways and end on arrangement. The stretches of wall in the upper section are reinforced with ashlars.

The length of the dam effectively extends the length of the river bank, although nowadays only that in the area of the Alcazaba remains visible, raised as it is above this wall's sturdy foundations. We know approximately where the dam finished, upriver of the Arab fortress at the exit to the present day calle de Atarazanas, where there was a road which exited via a gate in the no longer visible wall, leading to the river. The entire stretch of water beneath the bridge remains. Next to the bridge, at the entrance to the town, a wall can be seen with reinforced ashlar facings, similar to those

Etching of the Albarregas bridge and the "Los Milagros" aqueduct.

The Cornalvo reservoir.

of this construction, which probably signifies the existence of a ramp which led to a perimeter road which ran between the dam itself and the walled defence which was located, according to Moreno de Vargas, the chronicler, "only a stones throw away" from the dam.

Examples of dams such as the one in Mérida are well known in the Roman world, like the one in Rome itself and which new excavations have revealed, also existed along the Tiber. Other sites include London, Toulouse and perhaps that of *Ceasaraugusta* (now Zaragosa).

WATER SUPPLY SYSTEMS AQUEDUCTS AND RESERVOIRS

The Roman's utilitarian approach was demonstrated by the infrastructure in *Augusta Emerita,* with as many as three water supply systems, the ruins of which have been for the most part preserved and these alone demonstrate the effort made to provide the new colony's inhabitants with a plentiful supply of water as befitted the splendour presiding over Mérida's skilful urban planning.

The "Cornalvo" aqueduct

Aqua Augusta, the first water supply system, named as such on an inscription conserved in the Museum, is now known by the name of "Cornalvo", since it originated from the reservoir of this name *(caput aquae),* located 16 kilometres northeast of the town.

Two aspects (below, the inside)
of the Rabo de Buey-San Lázaro specus, or conduit.

———————— ℳ ————————

Located here is the preserved dam, extensively rebuilt as a result of modification projects carried out at the beginning of the last century, the purpose of which was to take advantage of the reservoir with its perimeter of almost 10km, for irrigation purposes and other such uses. The aforementioned modifications eventually camouflaged its original appearance. The retaining wall extended 220 metres between two gentle hills. Rising as it did to 18 metres in height, in the form of a slope, better able to withstand the force of the waters, comprising a powerful concrete structure, filled with earth, with the facing in ashlars.

Visible in the centre of the dam and for the most part submerged, is a square tower, 9.50 m wide and 20 m high, where the channel's control floodgates are located. The construction facings are in shaped granite blocks, the courses of which are laid lengthways and end on of a similar structure to those we have seen on other monuments in Mérida. A granite stone arch supported the walkway which linked the tower to the dam and although the cited parts have been preserved, the arch has been substituted by an unsightly metal structure.

The water channel started from the base of the tower through a well constructed tunnel 1.70m high and 0.70 m wide.

400 metres on from its outlet, it receives the supply from another, fast flowing, conduit which is sourced at "El Borbollón", a spot 3km to the north, in the Mirandilla mountains and which was probably that which originally supplied the city, before the reservoir itself was constructed and which appears to correspond to illustrations depicted on certain issues of Mérida's coins. Of this conduit, practically all is conserved of its course through the cultivated lands, the galleria constructed in dry-stone with a half barrel vaulted roof.

The aqueduct passed through Mérida's agricultural lands, mainly following the course of the river Albarregas (the former *Barraeca*) and on to the city. Various imponderables, such as water courses and valley floors were spanned by the construction of arcades and other stone built constructions in some cases, and in other cases by making corrections to the courses in search of the most favourable, which, in truth, are winding. Significant remains are conserved, almost in Mérida, next to the Psychiatric Hospital, which go by the expressive name of "Caño Quebrado", meaning crooked stream.

After covering a distance of around 25 kilometres, the conduit reached the city's eastern limits; crossed a necropolis, the industrial zone of "Los Bodegones" and penetrated the walled part of the city by the Municipal Stadium and the "Giner de los Rios" Public School. Considerable sections of the conduit have been discovered in this area with the vaulted roof intact, heading in the direction of the Theatre and Amphitheatre which it supplied. The main however, continued in a westerly direction, in line with the city wall, until finally coming to the Plaza de Toros where it apparently linked up with the site of the huge water tank *(castellum aquae)*.

The "Rabo de Buey-San Lázaro" aqueduct

The second water channel, known in modern times by the name of "Rabo de Buey-San Lázaro", originated from some 5 kilometres north of the city, where there existed various subterranean springs and water currents, on the land belonging to three properties, "Casa Herrara", "Las Tomas" and "Valhonde" which, conveniently channelled, constituted the main supply for this waterway.

Two views of the Rabo de Buey-San Lázaro aqueduct.

— ℳ —

The aqueduct's 4km route comes to us reasonably well preserved, the vestiges of which are truly spectacular. The main arcaded structure through which the water ran is above 2.50 metres high carefully constructed in dry-stone with half barrel vaults achieved by converging courses of the same material. In order to clean the channel, every so often there was a place containing a square inlet *(spiramina)*, surrounded by granite ashlars, together with an indent in which to place a ladder. The channel *(specus)*, strictly speaking, is 0.60m wide and appears to be lined by a layer of hydraulic mortar.

Above, the specus, right, general view of the Proserpina-Los Milagros aqueduct.

M

The channel comes out at the "La Godina" property and continues on to the "Rabo de Buey" water deposit where there presumably existed a sediment chamber for any impurities *(piscine limaria)*.

The entire length of the channel, from its origins, was repaired at the end of the 19th century, in order for the water to continue to flow as far as the city, as in Roman times, which thanks to the will of D. Pedro María Plano, at the time the local Mayor and reputable erudite, continued to be the case until the end of the nineteen seventies. Problems caused by the wide expanse of the Albarregas valley were overcome by the construction of elevated arches which linked the channel's supporting pillars. The construction was magnificent, almost a kilometre long, although nowadays there only remains three support pillars and some granite masonry arches, the details of which are comparable with those to be seen on the "Los Milagros" aqueduct, later described. Beneath the aqueduct stretched the road which united *Emerita* with *Toletum* (Toledo) and *Corduba* (Córdoba).

In the area of what is known as the "Casa del Anfiteatro", there appears an interesting decantation and water distribution tower, of a rectangular design, made up of a mixture of ashlars, dry-stone and brickwork with the arch facings also in brick. On the inside, the walls

were also decorated with paintings. The maximum height of the construction is 4.80 m and its width 2.30 m.

A number of pipes led from this water deposit tank: one towards the centre of the colony, the route of which can be seen in the Museo Nacional de Arte Romano, another towards an apparently industrial zone, to the North, and lastly, one in the direction of the Amphitheatre.

The Proserpina Water Supply System and "Los Milagros" Aqueduct.

Lastly, the third water supply system, known by the name of "Proserpina-LosMilagros", is the one of which the most significant remains have been preserved.

Its origin was in "Albuera de Carija", as it was known, and which, following the 18th century discovery of a memorial dedicated to the goddess, adopted the name of Proserpina. This reservoir is located 5 kilometres north of the city, accessed via a road which, although only narrow, is surfaced and starts from the crossroads which link Mérida with Montijo.

In this basin, with its five kilometre perimeter, water was collected both from rainfall and nearby rivers such as "Las Adelfas" and "Las Pardillas". To

Proserpina reservoir.

make best use of this source, notable canalization works were carried out which are still apparent today, although their original virtues have been diminished by 20th century modifications carried out in the forties.

The engineering work in this dam has some interesting features. As in the case of the previously mentioned "Cornalvo", it is comprised of a strong earth barrier and sloping dam with a concrete core and ashlar facings.

The dam itself is around 500 metres long, the height of which is 7 metres above the normal water level. The reliability of the dam wall and its structure was guaranteed by means of rectangular shaped buttresses which were higher than that of the dam wall, the present day appearance of which is for the most part down to reconstruction work undertaken in the 17th century. Two square turrets adjoining the dam wall provide access, via steps, down to the bottom where the floodgates are located.

Numerous details of the dam's construction came to light, during three reinforcement projects, undertaken some years ago by the Confederación Hidrográfica del Guadiana. Once the reservoir was emptied, with the water below its normal level, the full extent of the almost semi circular floodgates could be appreciated, very different from those constructed in the time of Felipe III, with water outfalls and retaining walls against the land providing reinforcement.

It was also possible to ascertain the existence of some considerable granite quarrying, its use by the Romans very much in evidence, and the source of the ashlars used in the construction of the bridge and numerous official buildings in the colony's early years. All these factors will be available to the numerous visitors who come to see this prime example of Roman hydraulic technology in the Centro de Interpretación del Agua, shortly to be inaugurated by the town council.

Coming back to the water supply channel, this extends some 9 km before reaching the city, seeking as it does, the best land level along the entire route to provide adequate landfall for the waters to flow readily.

For this purpose, with the aim of negotiating a considerable granite mass, the Romans had no qualms about constructing a tunnel *(cuniculus)* through the impressive stone mass to avoid having to make a costly detour around the same. The tunnel can be seen on the property by the name of "Cuarto de la Charca", which together with the adjacent properties "Carija" and "La Calera" provides a complete lesson in Roman hydraulic engineering, which in truth offers some extremely interesting solutions.

Elevated arcades were constructed to traverse the valley floors which have now disappeared save for the bases in the form of parapets.

The remains of the dry stone arcaded conduits are everywhere although there are sections such as that next to the road from Mérida to Motijo which have suffered considerable damage.

A good section of the conduit was recently discovered near to the municipal cemetery, the entire length of which has been prepared for public viewing.

Also in the "Santa Eulalia" district, ruins have been conserved of a settlement tank, with a sluicegate chamber and elevated outlet deposit *(piscina limaria),* from where the conduit began to rise to once more overcome the obstacle of the valley, this time that of Albarregas.

The length of the arcaded section from the aforementioned settlement tank to the existing terminal on the hill known as "El Calvario", is 827 metres with a maximum height of 25 metres.

This structure reveals the degree of perfection and mastery the Roman's acquired in providing solutions for this type of construction. It consists basically of a set of pillars the construction of which constitutes a strong concrete core with brick and ashlar facings, with five courses of each laid alternately. The pillars are 3 metres deep, every so often with a sloping buttress 2 metres wide and 2.50 metres long.

Each one is linked to another by means of brick built arches, although those which flank the current from the Albarregas are built of stone. The canal *(specus)* itself was built into the upper section of the arches.

This structure, which astonished Arab geographers and chroniclers who described it with fervour, and

Piscina Limaria and castellum acquae from Los Milagros water system.

that of the people of Mérida from former centuries, who considered it miraculous that the pillars still remained standing, from whence comes the name by which this aqueduct is known: "Los Milagros", meaning the miracles, having come this far in a good state of conservation. There still remains around 70 pillars which even though somewhat deteriorated, their monumental worth is perfectly enhanced by night time illumination, after the Theatre, the "Los Milagros" aqueduct, is considered the second most important monument in Mérida.

Some years ago strengthening and restoration work was carried out on some of the arches and the crowning cornice, which is clearly visible.

The water conduit came to an end in one of the city's eminent spots, the summit of "El Calvario", where at the start of the seventies remains were discovered which related to the structure of its deposit tank terminal to which another was added in the form of a monumental temple dedicated to

nymphs which is what can be seen today next to the hermitage Hermandad del Santísimo Cristo del Calvaria. On the inside it appears to be filled with marble covered staircases, constructed with alternating rows of ashlars and bricks.

The chronology of these conduits has been much debated traditionally being set around the time of Augustus, although the latest discoveries and advanced investigation techniques suggest this may have to be reviewed.

The "Cornalvo" conduit indisputably belongs to the Augustus period, on account of the preserved inscription which makes reference to the city's ancient name. There was an initial phase, to which we would have probably have likewise referred, supported only by "El Borbollón", to which others were added in the course of its trajectory. In a second phase, the supply was increased by the construction of the reservoir, something which happened, perhaps, in the final era of the emperors from the Julio-Claudia dynasty or in that of Flavius, since the construction of the floodgate towers would appear to correspond to this period.

The "Rabo de Buey-San Lázaro" aqueduct could be dated to either the Augustus period, or that of the early Julio-Claudia.

Lastly, the construction of the third of Mérida's water conduction systems "Proserpina-Los Milagros", had to have been end of the Flavius period or in Trojan times, since equally the data obtained from a study of the dam as features on the arch supporting pillars, with cyma recta cornices, like the arches themselves, which correspond to architectural details from this period.

THE ROMAN BATHS OF ALANGE

The eloquent remains of a substantial Roman baths complex found in the nearby town of Alange, 18 kilometres from Mérida have, on account of their merit, been duly declared a National Monument.

The spa, the name of which in ancient times was *Aquae,* was probably left abandoned in the Middle Ages, returning to its original use from the 18th century, new facilities having been constructed alongside the Roman remains which correspond to its present day structure.

The hot spring, the waters of which emerge at a temperature of 28° with a flow of 216 litres per minute, of an eminently therapeutic nature, of

The Roman Baths at Alange.

exceptional quality and with properties well renowned for patients suffering mainly from nervous illnesses, who come in significant numbers to take the waters during the spa season.

The spa's collection of buildings is spread over a wide area, which makes for a reasonable and pleasant stroll around the modern installations and the Roman building. The exterior appearance of the latter, being somewhat irregular, gives us absolutely no indication of the interior grandeur.

The Roman baths consist of a rectangular building, 33 metres long by 16 metres wide. The building is orientated from east to west with two incorporated rotundas.

A steep staircase, now attached to one of the buildings lesser sides, comes out at a corridor with a semi barrel vaulted ceiling along which the entrances to the bath chambers are found.

Both, still in use today, offer the same characteristics and dimensions: 10.90m in diameter with a height of 13.86m. In the centre, both have circular pools provided with descent steps. The vaulted roof in both cases is of a hemispheric dome, in the centre of which an oculus or circular hole has been made. The vaulted roofs were, in their time, decorated with paintings, vestiges of which were still visible at the end of the 18th century.

Distributed symmetrically on the walls of each room are four what appear to be apses or niches, the dimensions of which in some cases are feigned by the construction of brick partitions to make use of the space for changing rooms. Their original purpose was purely architectural, providing support for the vaulted roof.

In the spa's courtyard, next to the modern individual baths area, is a Votive altar which was dedicated to the goddess *Iuna Regina* by *Licinius Seranianus,* senator and probably governor of *Cappadocia* in the year 235, together with his wife *Varinia Etaccina,* for the health of their daughter *Varinia Serena*.

Next to the spa, the Cristo de los Baños hermitage, highly respected in the town and amongst bathers, was raised on what was possibly the site of a Roman cult, perpetuated in Visigoth times. The beautifully created image of Santísimo Cristo de los Baños, as it is named, is quite remarkable.

The spa could have been constructed in the 1st century AD, in the time of Flavius as indicated by certain features employed in its construction.

⋯ CHRISTIAN MÉRIDA ⋯

THE VISIGOTH COLLECTION

Installed in the Santa Clara convent church, site of the former Museo Romano, next to plaza de España, is a selection of examples from the Visigoth period which made up part of the collection from the old Museum. This exceptional collection will in due course be suitably exhibited in a museum which is currently in the planning stage.

Ancient *Emerita* lived a time of rare splendour starting from the end of the 5th century. The already firmly established religious power was the driving force behind the city's political, economical and social life, purposefully illustrated in an anonymous work from the period entitled *Vidas de los Santos Padres emeritenses*. It has been deduced from a study of the same that there existed an enriched and thriving culture, the wealth of which was founded on commercial activities maintained by the city with distant lands relating to the old Roman Empire.

The power of the church in Mérida was so great, with its eminent personalities: Paulo, Fidel and Massona, that until civil authority, in the time of king Leovigildo, the city had to abandon its objective of locating its administrative capital here and be resigned to continue in Toledo.

Not surprisingly this ambience was conducive to exceptional artistic activity which came to express

---

𝕸

Two niches from the Visigoth collection.

itself in a new form of art: Hispanic art from the Visigoth period.

The genesis of Visigoth art in Mérida contained various essential elements: the Hispano-Roman tradition, artistic themes fully expressed in the Constantinople region and others which, elaborated in the Byzantine world, have been reinterpretated by various Italic schools, mainly Ravenna and others, lastly those from Northern Africa, together with the strictly oriental elements which arrived here via the Byzantium route.

Mérida's flourishing community life during the Visigoth period is well evident, equally demonstrated by its archaeology

This collection is the most important of its kind on the Iberian Peninsula. The collection began to be put together in the 16th century to be continuously complemented by subsequent findings over the centuries in the city and by those resulting from the systematic excavations carried out mainly in the area of the Arab Citadel, in San Pedro de Mérida and in that of the "Casa Herrera" basilica.

Amongst the pieces, there are those of singular importance, arranged according to the area and structure of the nave.

The collection of relatively unknown architectural elements originating from various civil and religious buildings is worth mentioning since many of these objects reappeared incorporated within the city's modern constructions. Amongst which are pilasters, with their beautiful foliage decoration, capitals, and ogees corresponding to various centuries though mainly the 6th and 7th.

Worthy of a mention apart is the wrought iron work, with its various decorative motifs, plants and animals created by means of a distinct system of symbols, an excellent exponent of the quality workmanship in Mérida.

Various elements of the original liturgy have been preserved, such as altar supports, with the *loculus* or box to deposit relics, altar tables, such as that from the "Casa Herrera", bearing an inscription, as well as prismatic altar stones for the deposition of relics.

Among these inscriptions, a good many memorial stones, using the expressions of the time, mention the names of the deceased and the date of their demise.

Other inscriptions mention buildings and churches, such as that referring to the consecration of that of Santa María and of all the Virgins, in which a good number of religious relics have been conserved, amongst which are those of Santiago and the Cruz del Señor, or Lord's Cross.

Other relevant pieces such as the niche in the form of a scalloped vaulted arch, decorated with a Roman emperor's standard with a crucifix from which hang the letters Alpha and Omega and a baptismal font from the 6th century AD complete this impressive testimonial collection from the time of the Visigoths.

A range of ceramic utensils are displayed in glass cabinets, the morphology of which is varied (jugs, terracotta lamps decorated with Christian symbols), metallic pieces, plaques with bas-reliefs and decorated bricks.

THE CASA HERRERA EARLY CHRISTIAN BASILICA

The basilica, located some 7km north of Mérida, set on a minor hill, the slopes of which are slightly inclined towards the south and west (38° 55' north and 2° 37' west), was discovered and partially excavated in 1943 by J. de C. Serra Rafols. Its documentation and cleaning work was later undertaken by T. Ulbert and in 1971-1972, accompanied by L. Caballero Zoreda, the excavation works which represent the monument as we see today.

The temple had three aisles of an almost square design, a little narrower on the west side, separated by six slightly banked columns, the end ones very close to the triumphal arch of the apses which juts out on the extremes of the east-west axis.

The construction is based on dry stone-walls, with some brickwork, cemented on two faces by a thin layer of mortar, between which was placed a rather more contemptible substance. Some sections of the foundations contained

Screen from the Visigoth collection.

granite ashlars, as do the corners. The total length of the building is 34 metres and at its widest point, on the east side 22 metres.

The building can be divided into two sections: the basilica with its three aisles and the adjoining annexes.

The basilica presented an eastern apse of 5.50 metres long by 5 metres wide; that of the west, for its part, measuring only 4.75 by 4.65 metres. The central aisle which narrowed from east to west (5.35 to 4.65 metres) was separated from the lateral aisles by 12 white single piece marble columns, set on three tier Corinthian bases some of which can be found "in situ". On the north lateral aisle, the entrance can still be seen intact, flanked by a wall of ashlars, and on the floor the marmoreal threshold, preserved in its original site.

The adjoining annexes are comprised of seven small cubicles of approximately 4 by 4 metres, significantly modified by successive renovation work carried out on the building, the purpose of which has yet to be defined in some cases, though they were without doubt related to the basilica's liturgical services. Worth pointing out is that located northeast of the basilica, in which baptisms were performed and which displays two different phases; the first in which a deep rectangular font was used and the second in which two small adjoining fonts were added.

The entire floor originally of ceramic tiles, some sections later being replaced by *opus signum;* was literally destroyed by the burials which took place inside the basilica from the 6th century onwards.

On the whole, from the excavation work, it has been possible to ascertain the basilica was constructed, with its apses opposite ways on, around 500 AD, the existence of two clearly defined construction phases much in evidence. The first, in which the basilica with its three aisles was constructed, with the apses opposite ways on and the aisles separated by columns, and the second phase, in which the baptistery and the annexed buildings were constructed perhaps already into the second half of the 6th century.

Casa Herrera Basilica.

XENODOCHIUM

One of the most remarkable monuments conserved in Mérida is that discovered a few years ago next to the Santa Eulalia church, close to where one of the roman roads passed which departed from the colony's northern gate. On top of the pre-existing remains of a late imperial necropolis, in the second half of the 6th century a refuge was raised for pilgrims. It was at the personal initiative of the bishop Masona, a citizen of Mérida who left one of the biggest impressions during his episcopacy, as is related in the short work from the 7th century "About the Life and Miracles of the Holy Fathers of Mérida", in which there appears news of this cited charitable institution. Masona, a bishop with saintly qualities, was a man with proven Christian charity, a fact clearly demonstrated by founding this refuge for pilgrims and beggars around the year 580.

In the time of the Visigoths it was usual that beggars and unknowns who came to Christian towns took sanctuary in the churches, their porticos, monasteries and other religious places. In reality the, biggest attraction for beggars, the poor and the pilgrims were the large sanctuaries which housed the tomb or relics of saints. Other places of interest for beggars were the poorhouses or *xenodochia*. The majority of which were Episcopal foundations.

They have on occasions, been known to be monastic or secular foundations, such as the

Xenodochium.

xenodochium in Lyon founded in 549 by king Childeberto and queen Ultragotha, although always under rule of Episcopal power. Unlike the eastern hospitals and poorhouses which provided sanctuary for the sick, lepers, the poor, the old, women in labour, widows and orphans, these were specifically for the poor and pilgrims. For the most part they were buildings of limited capacity. The *xenodochium* constructed by Bishop Cesario is Arles was no more than a *domus spatiosisssima* and that of Reims, at the beginning of the 6th century, only accommodated twelve unknowns, the number of which is repeated since it is in direct relation to the twelve apostles. The *xenodochium* constructed at the beginning of the 7th century by Adalgisel, deacon of the church of Verdun, was able to shelter

sixteen needy. Built for this exceedingly strange cause was this lavish *xenodochium* in Mérida, with its richly carved marble pilasters, now preserved in the Visigoth Collection in the Museo Nacional de Arte Romano. It could only be explained by the lavish material in the church of Mérida itself, which came to be legendary in the time of the Visigoths.

The building was of a rectangular outline, accessed by a doorway which opened onto a central area, both sides of which ran long arcaded passages separated by patios. The two wings, to the north and south of the central aisle, are symmetrical. Only one of the two has been fully preserved, since the other remains hidden beneath the railway tracks which pass through here. Not forgetting these were symmetrical and 17 metres long by 2.40 metres wide.

The *xenodochium,* as in other known examples, would have had a second floor, in which the bedrooms were located.

··· MUSLIM MÉRIDA ···

THE ALCAZABA

The city's Arab monument, par excellence: the Alcazaba or citadel is located very close to Plaza de España, in the area south of the old town, beyond the limits of the river Guadiana, which provided it with a natural source of defence.

Actually a fortification in the form of a quadrilateral, the sides of which measure between 132 and 137 metres, surrounded by walls covering a perimeter of 538 metres with an average thickness of 2.70 metres. The basic elements used in its construction consists of granite ashlars, the majority of which came from old Roman buildings, arranged as they were in two courses between which was an abundant filling based on ashlars, mortar and earth.

Square towers were erected at regular intervals, up to a total of 25, which in the sections best preserved reach a height of 15 metres. Accessed as it was by at least three gateways, the present day entrance is actually the product of mutilation from the current century. Intended to defend the nearby bridge is an adjoining smaller enclosure 20 by 23 metres, with four gateways, beneath which, recent excavations have revealed traces of the original Roman gateway which guaranteed entry to the city from this point, with a double access road, as corresponds to the gateway depicted on local coins from the periods of Augustus and Tiberius.

A marble memorial stone placed above the gate which gave entry to the fortress from the bridge tells us something of its construction.

Martín Almagro wrote:

"In the name of Allah, the Clement, the Merciful. The blessing of Allah and protection to all those who show obedience to Allah".

Two views of the Alcazaba.

"This fortress and thus the fortification is to be constructed, as a place of refuge for those subjects under his obedience, the emir Ab de Rahman, son of Al Haken, glorified by Allah, beneath the guidance of his architect Abd Allah, son of Kulaid, son of Tálaba and Gaifar , son of Mukassir, his freedman, director of the construction, in the month of rabbi 11, of the year 220 (835 of the Christian Era)"

reinforced in its most vulnerable places, perhaps belatedly, with strong granite ashlars.

On the left is the most significant monument of all, the Alijibe, commonly known as the "baño de la reina", the queen's bath. Possibly of Roman origin and which continuously supplied the fortress with water by means of filtrations from the adjacent Guadiana; its present day appearance is the work

View of the Alcazaba.

The tour begins by passing through the artificial gate open in the wall opposite the river. Taking a footpath which leads gently down towards the river, to our left are the vestiges of a sumptuous Roman mansion from late imperial times, set between two urban roads.

There still remains preserved some decorative tiling and a splendid room panelled with coloured marble (*opus sectile*) which gives some idea of the importance of the excavations carried out in the seventies by don José Alvarez Sáenz de Buruaga, and more recently those by the Junta de Extremadura.

Once along the paved roman road we come to the original town wall, a solid dry stone structure,

of the Arabs, who used an abundance of Roman and Visigoth material in their construction. Accessed as it is along paths made up of Visigoth marble pilasters, decorated with foliage and which lead towards a landing, where new pilasters, this time serving as jambs and lintels guide the way, by means of a double staircase which would have enabled the cavalry to descend to the lower level of the tank, on a level with the river, protected by a magnificent dome in granite ashlars of Roman origin, which helped to support a beautiful Visigoth pilaster finished with a capital from late Imperial times.

The visit can be completed by ascending the walls, from where the Roman bridge can be viewed in its entire length, and in particular the section from the time of Augustus, which finishes at the first ramp.

We can also appreciate beneath our feet, the strong roman dyke which protected the city from the river's floodwaters, a solid dry stone structure added to which is the outer facing of the Arab wall along its entire length.

The construction, in bygone years buried beneath modern buildings (until the seventies it

𝔐

Alcazaba. View with the bridge and the Centro Cultural.

was a market garden) is gradually retrieving its original appearance thanks to the expropriation documents for the terraced houses on the outside and the systematic archaeological excavation work carried out on the inside, which is still ongoing, certain to reveal, in addition to a fair stretch of the original city walls, a residential quarter from late Roman times and possibly some civil or ecclesiastical Visigoth construction.

We can complete the visit by taking a look, in the northwest corner, at the convent raised by the gentlemen of the Orden de Santiago after the city was recaptured by Alfonso IX in 1228, who adapted this part of the district firstly for the house

belonging to this religious Order and later for the Convent. To this was added the beautiful Torre de Homenaje, with its cloisters set on two floors with semicircular arches raised over columns on a simple base, with smooth shafts and in some cases Ionic capitals; a church and some outbuildings. The entire complex was severely damaged during the battles between the supporters of Isabel la Católica and Juana la *Beltraneja,* the skirmishes between Soult and Wellington as well as at the start of the civil war. Following extensive restoration work, the Convent is now the headquarters of the district council, the Junta de Extremadura, to which entry is gained via the plaza del Rastro.

··· Modern Mérida ···

BASÍLICA DE SANTA EULALIA

The basilica was erected, according to belief, at the beginning of the 4th century, in the place where Santa Eulalia surrendered to martyrdom during the Diocleciano persecution (304). The original structure was ardently praised in the poetic words of Prudencio, in his work entitled *Peristephanon* (adorned with astonishing marbles, covered with golden roofs and proudly exhibiting rich mosaics, like a glorious flower filled meadow). Subsequent modifications carried out by the Archbishop Fidel (560-571) were similarly related by Paulo Diácono in his work on the Fathers of Mérida, of which, Muslim rule was determined to erase every last vestige.

The present day appearance generally corresponds to the reconstruction work carried out in the 13th century, after the city was conquered by the Christian Army in 1230. Of the original and basic Romanesque construction, their remains the floorplan, the typical basilica, with

Santa Eulalia Basilica.

three aisles, the central one being the largest, without any indication of crossing in the layout, with three apses at the top, semicircular on the inside and squared on the outside. From this first period also comes one of the main entrances from the south façade, which connects the crossing with the west façade, created by an opening with a horseshoe shaped arch with archivolts of the same form, supported by marble pillars. The west façade, now walled in by the adjacent convent, bears the same characteristics as the former, though more stylised, resembling those which access the lateral apses.

The interior is supported by four huge central buttresses, two cylindrical and two in the shape of a cruciform, to which are attached four columns with capitals, from different eras, all of which supports the pointed arches. As for the roof, the wooden sections from the second and third phase (16th C) are mixed with the ribbed and cross barrel vaulted ceilings from the Gothic period.

The presbytery, which appears also to be from this same period, is framed by a grand ogival arcade supported by two large columns with roman capitals, above which opens a Romanesque window.

Inside there now remains only a chapel by the side of that of the Epistle and another two at the sides of the choir stalls.

Of the modifications made to the church in later times, worthy of some attention is the wooden roof in the central section before the choir stalls, which still has its chamfered Mudejar framework, as well as the second part of the south façade, from the Isabel period (16th C) which is in two sections: the lower, with an entrance doorway opening onto a tri-lobular arch

Santa Eulalia. The Bishops Crypt.

Santa Eulalia. The San Martin Chapel.

and the upper, an entrance onto a semicircular arch framed by a fine moulded surround.

From the altarpieces and sculptures in the church, we can make out the image of the Santísimo Cristo de los Remedios, from the 16thC Castilian school, and that of Nuestro Padre Jesús Nazareno, attributed to the 18th C school of Granada.

The archaeological excavations

In order to replace the floor in the church, a series of archaeological interventions have been made on behalf of the district council's Education and Culture department, which has announced an impressive archaeological programme to help to clear up more than a few mysteries regarding the history of the original church.

Research carried out until now confirms that the earliest remains found in the excavations date back to Roman times, belonging to either a private house or a bath house of which there remains vestiges of basins, cisterns and tiling, and which occupy almost the entire area taken up by the present day church. Corresponding to the early Christian period (4th C and 5th C) are two mausoleums, one of which still retains on its ceiling the remains of early mosaic decoration, around which are smaller buildings possibly places of worship related to the early Christian martyrs, as in the case of Santa Eulalia, to which one of them

may be related. On to the Visigoth period, from whence came the strong granite ashlar foundations, which in theory are from the basilica's extension carried out by Archbishop Fidel and spoken of in the writings of Deacon Paulo and also the abundant remains of sarcophagi and marble plaques from sepulchres as well as the remains of another mausoleum with a mosaic and a banqueting table.

The Santa Eulalia Basílica Study Centre

It was precisely the enormous impact caused by finding the historic archaeological remains beneath the basilica, which brought about the idea of sharing the unavoidable cultural use of the church, by suitably displaying the remains and subsequently opening to the public. On this basis, a type of archaeological crypt was built, not without some difficulty, since it was precisely for this reason the church floor was raised in certain places, and significant strengthening and tiling work was carried out, which enabled us to ascertain the basilica's original layout and study the apse, originating as it did from the Visigoth church and concealed until that time by altarpieces and minor works. It is without doubt a feat of understanding to see the historic transformation of this place, the construction within this ancient sacristy of a modern study centre.

Convento de Santa Olalla.

A visit to the anteroom before the crypt helps to explain the importance of the remains conserved "in situ" in the adjacent crypt: the Santa Eulalia burial mound, the bishops Crypt, the San Martín mausoleum-chapel, the burial site of the Archdeacon Eleuterio, etc. The evolution this place has undergone is recreated by a small exhibition of remains from the site's various stages of occupation, together with an abundance of explanatory notice boards covering the important role played by Merida's Saint during the city's historic transformation and diorama achievements.

CONVENTO DE SANTA OLALLA

Adjacent to the church of the same name, including to that which walled in the original Roman gates at the foot of the same, is the sisters of Santa Eulalia convent. The convent was originally raised in its first phase of construction around 1530, and continued well into the 18th century. The main body of the building is of an L shaped construction, with the cloisters and rooms around the outside. A particularly beautiful feature is the enclosed balcony with Doric columns. The building's construction elements included stonework facades and arches, as well as reused materials and brick packed with

earth. The roof covering the most important areas (the east wing) is of a barrel arch form, the remaining being of wood. It was the occasional residence of the kings during their visits to the city, creating a somewhat precarious situation for the others until its convent status was removed during the alienation, when it passed into private hands to be used for other purposes, containing until only a few years ago a timber warehouse.

CONVENTO DE SAN ANDRÉS

This convent was constructed in 1571 at the wishes of Mérida's don Francisco de Vargas, although not actually completed until 1636. Of its original, much dilapidated and transformed structure, there remains only the church, now a shop, the entrance of which presides over plaza de Santo Domingo.

The baroque style church of a rectangular layout without, without the apse, measures 7.60 m by 16.65 m; the central part is covered by a barrel arched roof and with the same with an intersecting arch in the presbytery and the last section. The façade which faces onto the plaza de Santo Domingo, the best conserved, is of a brick construction covered with lime mortar, on a base of granite ashlars, in the centre of which projects and elegant granite entrance, of Tuscan order, with two columns either side of the doorway and perfect entablature of the cornice, on top of which is a vaulted niche with the marble image of Santo Domingo and the Order's coat of arms with the inscription: "Defendere Fidei ordo veritatis".

The convent was abandoned in frankly decadent times, after losing its religious status, adopting various civil roles and suffering considerable damage which reduced it to its present state; it was declared by Decree on the 10th of February 1989 to be of cultural interest in the hopes of a more respectable destiny, in keeping with its glorious past.

CONVENTO HOSPITAL DE JESÚS NAZARENO

Founded as it was around 1724, although construction work didn't finish until ten years later, by the Hermanos de Jesús from the Franciscan tertiary order which was created by one of the Fathers of Mérida, padre Cristóbal de Santa Catalina

in 1673, with the intention of attending to the convalescent sick without economic resources.

The chosen site was the small plaza de Santiago, using for materials, the surrounding scattered remains of which some were from the ancient Roman forum buildings and even some support structures from an old mosque, judging by the Arabic characters engraved on some of the columns in the cloisters. The convent hospital grew rapidly during the 18th century, a garden of antiquities also being created, known as the "Jardín de Antigüedades", at the hands of Friar Domingo de Nuestra Señora and which was to be the origins of the future Archaeological Museum. Nevertheless and owing to economic difficulties, it fell into a considerable state of disrepair at the start of the 19th century and was abandoned entirely during the War of Independence. Once this was over, restoration work began which only finished in 1837, but by 1839 it was abandoned definitively, falling under civil jurisdiction, to be used as an asylum and later a civil prison.

Of its original construction, now completely transformed by successive works which since 1929 have been carried out to make it a suitable Parador

Convento Hospital de Jesús Nazareno, now a Parador.

───────── ℳ ─────────

Nacional de Turismo, the best preserved part is that of the cloisters and the church, of a rectangular design with incipient crossing and three semicircular apses, with a cupola on pendentives and a lantern over the crossing.

The "Jardín de Antigüedades" garden

Halfway through the 18th century, Dr Forner and Segarra, the local doctor and father of the famous polemicist and writer Juan Pablo Forner, together with P. Domingo de Nuestra Sefiora, a monk from the Convento de Jésus, concerned by the deterioration and dispersal of Mérida's antiquities started the worthy undertaking of systematically collecting all the Roman and Visigoth pieces of interest. They decided to group the items together to be exhibited in an intentionally museum like fashion, in the Convento-Hospital de Jésus , mainly in its garden, from whence comes the poetic name "Jardín de Antigüedades".

This was undoubtedly a valuable archaeological collection, which includes the remains still conserved in the building today, made up of sculptures, architectural pieces and above all inscriptions, which to be seen at their best were built into the walls of the cited garden.

With time and given the many vicissitudes experienced by the convent, the collection was dispersed. Some inscriptions, which we know of thanks to the testimony of ancient writers, have disappeared. Those which weren't robbed or disfigured were moved, at the end of the 19th century to the new archaeological museum which was being set up.

The pieces which in their day formed part of the Archaeological Collection in the "Jardín de Antigüedades" are currently preserved in the same building in which they were initially deposited and in Mérida's Museo Nacional de Arte Romano.

Dispersed throughout the garden are various

———————— ℳ ————————

Two views of the "Jardín de Antigüedades" garden.

Entrance to the Iglesia del Carmen.

———————— ℳ ————————

architectural pieces constructed in marble and local stone. Remarkable pieces include part of a statue, cornices from the forum's portico, capitals and some bases from marble columns, the significant diameter of which tells us they formed part of important public Roman buildings. Other bases, for their part, were cut at right angles and bore mountings for bolts since they were reused to hold one of the convent's doors.

As far as the granite pieces are concerned, their chronology extends from the period the city was founded, under the rule of Emperor Augustus (cornices), to the modern period (capitals from columns and pilasters), the latter possibly from the parish church of Santiago, demolished only a few years before the construction of the Convento-Hospital de Jésus Nazareno, the architectural pillaging of which was incorporated in its construction.

IGLESIA DE NUESTRA SEÑORA DEL CARMEN

Mérida's 18th century religious architecture is well represented by this church founded by the Orden de San Francisco. In the shape of a Latin cross, of which the nave is covered by a barrel

Entrance to the Convento de Concepcionistas.

Cristo de la O, in Santa Maria Cathedral.

vaulted ceiling with a cupola on the crossing. The most outstanding feature of this church is the façade, of Tuscan order, with two shaped pilasters and a Doric frieze decorated with triglyphs and metopes, from where the second section begins which houses a split façade of Ionic order, crowned with busts and a central coat of arms. The niche with the image of the Virgen con el Niño, the virgin and child is flanked by the coat of arms from the church's religious Order and that of Mérida itself, above which runs a decorative scalloped trim. A memorial stone bears the following inscription: "The first stone for this church and convent was laid on the 26th April 1721 and all completed the holy saints were put in place on the 19th October 1737. For the glory of Christ and his virgin mother. Amen".

The interior is rather austere, and the 19th century neoclassic altarpieces are of dubious artistic worth, likewise the collection of sculptures.

CONVENTO DE M. M. CONCEPCIONISTAS

The convent of the dedicated nuns and order of the Limpia Concepción de Nuestra Señora was founded by don Francisco Moreno de Almaraz in 1588, the nuns having taken care of him, coming as he did from Llerena,

The church, of a rectangular layout, is covered with a barrel vaulted roof intersected with a cupola on pendentives in some form of crossing, aslo in the presbytery. On the outside of the church, one main section of the façade presents two entrances with lintels, belonging to the convent at the base of which are the only two opening doors to the same.

The stonework sections correspond to the building's early days, with an arched entrance with foliage mouldings on its leans, defined by half-relief columns which support an entablature with a scalloped niche containing the image of the Virgin and Child.

Santa Maria Church.

CONCATEDRAL DE SANTA MARÍA

The Santa María church is raised where in the Visigoth period another homonymy was constructed, that of Merida's city cathedral. The cathedral completely destroyed, some of its features are known thanks to its brief description in the precious short work previously cited from the 7th century AD entitled "The Life and Miracles of the Holy Fathers of Mérida". Mérida's cathedral was the seat of ecumenical council and also held the denomination of Santa Jerusalén. It included a *basilicula* or small attached baptistery and an *episcopium* or Episcopal palace.

When the city of Mérida fell under Muslim power, Christian cults were respected, but as time went on, the church fell into a state of absolute abandon and was finally demolished. At the beginning of the 13th century, when the city was recaptured by Christian troops, the former religious devotion was readopted and the church rebuilt from its foundations,

presenting what we see today, although of a very different appearance.

The church contains three aisles, the central one being twice the width of those to the sides, separated by square shaped pillars, with a half-relief column on the front of each above which rise pointed arches. The aisles ceilings, originally a Mudejar framework, are now in the form of a groin vault.

The presbytery is divided into two sections, the first of a rectangular distribution and the second like a fan, covered by trussed vaulted ceilings with keystones each decorated with a rosette and the Cordero Místico, or Lamb of God.

Both sides of the presbytery, beneath the canopied arches are the alabaster sepulchres of don Diego de Vera y Mendoza, of the Orden de Santiago and his wife doña Marina Gómez de Figueroa.

The central apse is adorned with a huge altarpiece from 1762. Divided as it is into two sections, the top having been removed in modern times to reveal a 13th century window.

The central niche on the second section, supported by a set of pedestals, contains the image of the patron saint of the church accompanied by apostles Pedro and Pablo and Mérida's patron saints, Eulalia and Julia.

Of the apse chapels, particularly worthy of note is that of the Epístola, or Epistle, that of the condes de la Roca, divided into two parts, both of which are covered by ribbed vaults one of the keystones displaying the elaborate coat of arms of the patrons of the same. In the chapel next to that of the Evangelio or Gospel, is the impressive sculpture of Cristo de la O, a magnificent representation of 14th century imagery.

Amongst the funeral chapels, worthy of mention is that of doña Cecilia de Mendoza, from the first third of the 16th century and also the one built at the request of Mérida's conquistador Moreno de Almaraz.

The eastern façade, at the foot of the church, is the work of maestro Mateo Sánchez de Villaviciosa. It consists of two main sections; the lower, with double moulded pilasters of the Ionic order, and the upper, with fluted Corinthian pilasters which frame the coat of arms from the religious orders of both Mérida and Santiago.

Both display tablatures, that of the second section being finished by an eave, above which opens a doorway with lintel and a small balcony. On the tablature is the psalm of David: Domum tuam Domine Sanctitudo. Ps.LXXXII".

The church's south façade, on to the plaza, is down to the pious initiative of Moreno de Almaraz and was completed in 1579. The alabaster statue of Nuestra Señora de la Guía, was dedicated to travellers, mainly in this case, those who went to the Indies.

EL PALACIO DE MENDOZA

The only remaining palace in Mérida disappeared at the end of the last century, being that of the Counts and later the Dukes of la Roca, which in its day belonged to don Luis de Mendoza, who married a lady from the Vera family, to whom, in reality, the building belonged.

With two orientated south facades looking over the plaza, being the main façade and that to the west, it was constructed from reused Roman ashlars from two clearly distinguished periods.

— ℳ —

*Exterior view of
Mendoza Palace.*

Constructed in the 15th century, it has a beautiful window with three bi-lobular arches and marble mullions with small emblems on capitals which speaks of late Gothicism as do the two smaller arched windows. The façade was remodelled some time towards the end of the 16th century or the beginning of the 17th century in keeping with the times, with a long balcony with three widows complete with lintels with two curved pediments flanking one of a triangular form divided at its peak to accommodate a coat of arms representing the Vera family and alliances.

The coat of arms is displayed on the breast of an eagle which holds in its beak a parchment bearing the inscription "Varitas Vincit", being the motto adopted by the army of los condes de la Roca. The pediments are finished with globes, pyramids and trees.

Beneath the Gothic window is a door, which could well be the palace's original, now a large window. The pediment is finished in volutes and the coat of arms on the eagle displays the arms from the Vera, Tovar, Zúñiga and Ovando families. It contains, as does the other coat of arms, the cross of Santiago.

The much reformed interior contains a courtyard with cloistered passages, only one of which is of the original design, the three remaining having Tuscan columns, probably as a result of the 17th century modifications.

LA IGLESIA DE SANTA CLARA

The Santa Clara church was founded as a convent for nuns from the order of Santa Clara by its patron, doctor Lope Sánchez de Triana, in the year 1602 and working on its construction was the famous rogue Estebanillo González.

Built of alternating squares of brick and dry stonework, with the exception of the gables at the ends of the church, of which all is in dry stonework,

Of the windows, the plinths, façades and frames are all in granite, some blocks of which still display the marks left by the stonemasons.

The east portal, of Tuscan order, is made up of two columns which support an entablature with a divided pediment to take a niche which shelters the statue of Nuestra Señora de la Antigua, in other times in the convent of the same name. Above this niche is another architectural feature with pilasters supporting another

a tannery. What is visible today is almost exclusively from the gothic style church, built towards the end of the 16th century or the beginning of the 17th century, with walls constructed in poor masonry of a rectangular layout with a plain main façade.

The roof, perhaps the most interesting feature of all, is created by two star vaults supported by six pillars on the inside and six robust buttresses on the outside. It opens on to the outside on two facades

Iglesia de Nuestra Señora de la Antigua. Exterior.

divided pediment, occupied by a coat of arms with three heads of Christ and above the letters I H S.

The western portal, onto plaza de Santa Clara, is of a similar design, but simpler.

Exhibited inside the church is a valuable collection from Merida's Visigoth period.

ERMITA DE NUESTRA SEÑORA DE LA ANTIGUA

This chapel was originally part of the old monastery founded around 1676 by the barefoot Franciscan monks, of the same name. Already abandoned by the first half of the 18th century, what was left of the monastery at first housed a wool washhouse and later

that at the foot of the church, with a tri-lobular arch finished in reinforced ashlars; and a second on the side of the Epistle, arched with fluting in the archivolt which continues on to the jambs. The portal is surrounded by an architrave which starts from the continuation of the last fluting on the jamb and a cornice, above which and at both ends are pinnacles, in the centre of each opens a doorway with a lintel beneath another cornice. The façade is finished with brickwork cresting.

The building today, following its acquisition by the local council, houses a cultural centre.

*Exterior and interior
of the Extremadura
Assembly.*

— 𝔐 —

THE FORMER HOSPITAL OF SAN JUAN DE DIOS AND SEAT OF THE EXTREMADURA ASSEMBLY

What is today the headquarters of the Asamblea de Extremadura, was in the past a hospital, run by brothers from the Orden Hospitaleria de San Juan de Dios. Its origins are of a former religious order, dedicated to Nuestra Señora de la Piedad. The building in question underwent a significant transformation in the second half of the 18th century, according to the words of the epigraph on the building's main façade. Later, on account of the War of Independence, the building suffered substantial damage, though remaining in service until the time ecclesiastical properties were disentailed. It was left abandoned by the Community in the year 1838. In the 20th century it came to retrieve its former health care role, being run this time by nuns, the Hermanas de la Caridad de San Vincente de Paúl, until its definitive conversion as the headquarters of Extremadura's political body.

In reality there remains little of the building's original appearance. The façade has lost its bell gable and the roof was replaces by a cupola. The cornice eaves contain allegories from the provinces of Extremadura. Notable features on the inside include the cloister and, decorating the wall of the chamber, a Roman mosaic from Mérida's Museum. The mosaic's central scene depicts a wild boar being hunted, pursued by a pack of hounds, within a conventional countryside setting expounded by the presence of three bushes. This hunting theme is further testified in similar mosaics discovered in the Italic peninsula, North Africa and the Iberian Peninsula itself. The style of the mosaic is not of an excessively high technical quality, though it can be dated to the start of the 5th century AD.

LA PLAZA DE TOROS

The Fiesta Nacional, as it is named, has deep roots in Mérida similar to those of other towns and cities in Spain. Initially the bull fights were held in an improvised fashion in the Plaza, but in the last quarter of the 18th century a strange discovery was made in the then named "old amphitheatre", non

Mérida's Plaza de Toros.

other than the Roman theatre, for the most part buried and surrounded by a wall to create a bullring for the bullfighting. The present day bullring, one of the best of its time, began to be constructed in 1902, in one of the city's most prominent sites, where there stood in modern times, a chapel dedicated to San Albín and San Gregorio mentioned by the city's chronicler, Bernabé Moreno de Vargas. When excavations began, sculptures and marmoreal inscriptions were discovered from a temple dedicated in Roman times to eastern gods, the reason for which it was thought there was a shrine dedicated to Mitre in this place, mentioned elsewhere in this guide.

The inaugural bullfight was held in the new plaza de toros or bullring, on the 5th July 1914, the expectation so great that the Municipal Corporation had to issue an edict to regulate the traffic flow of carriages which would be coming to the city.

From a structural point of view, the plaza is set on three levels with many large windows with a

crenellated main entrance. The interior was substantially modified on the occasion of reform work which unfortunately caused the Mudejar roofs over the stands to disappear.

The bullring's capacity rose to eight thousand six hundred and eighty five seats, counting all the sections typical of this type of construction.

THE LUSITANIA BRIDGE

Said to be something of a challenge for the company to construct a third bridge over the river Guadiana,, on account of its size, the surrounding landscape and above all, its proximity to the exceptional roman bridge, in the words of creator, architect, civil engineer and sculptor, Valencian born, Santiago Calatrava Valls. The construction of this bridge made it possible to close the ancient roman bridge to traffic, resulting in it having been exclusively for pedestrian use for two thousand years. On the modern bridge, given the name of Lusitania as homage to the capital of this ancient Roman province, the relation between pedestrians and vehicles has been taken into account, the central section being raised 1.50 metres, in such a

The Lusitania bridge.

way that pedestrians not only gain with regard to safety but also have an excellent view over the whole and its surroundings. The width is similar to that of its roman counterpart.

The bridge is 512.5 metres long with a large central arc with a 202.5 metre span with four intermediate stretches of 52.5 metres with one at either end of 50 metres. The transversal section is made up of two roads, each 7 metres wide, and a central walkway of a little more than 6 metres wide. Consequently the bridge is divided into three well defined sections: The first, from its start to the central arch, which runs a length of 200 metres; the intermediate section, with its spectacular arc, 30 metres high, secured by stays and open at the sides to lighten the costs and help to blend the structure into its surroundings and finally, the third section, identical to the first and next to the roundabout presided over by the replica of the statue of the very famous Augosto de Primaporta. The bridge piles, for their part, are

of a hydrodynamic design, minimising the section and reducing the heavy appearance in accordance with that specified in the original construction project. The beginnings of the bridge are, on both banks, combined with urban elements such as traffic islands, ramps and stairways.

The Puente de la Lusitania was inaugurated on the 10th of December 1991.

Different views of modern Mérida. From top to bottom and from left to right: Plaza de España, Palacio de Congresos (conference centre), la Biblioteca (the library), la Escuela de Administración Publica, the "Siete Sellos" park, and the Mercado de Abastos (market).

··· INDEX ···